SERPENT CLUB PRESS
# NEW WRITING
## FALL '23

Printed in the United States of America
Designed & Formatted by Anastasia Wolfe
Cover Image by Olivia van Kuiken

# TABLE OF CONTENTS

# Worcester Screws
Alexander Sammartino

I was supposed to staff a factory that turns human skeletons into tiny screws. The factory was in central Mass. The skeletons were donated by Science. These donated bones became screws, rods, plates, pins. There's no additional procedure if rather than a metal screw you've got one made of human bone sealing your fracture. Your broken self absorbs the matter of a stranger.

"Sorry about that," said Steve, the Amtrol supervisor, when I stepped inside his office. A protester had pegged me with a cup of Dunkin. There were about thirty of them, all waving signs and mumbling chants and marching about in the snow.

"That's a small fraction of those on the floor," Steve said. "Most are taking the shutdown on the chin."

"Hey, pal, don't worry about it." I wiped myself off with some napkins.

"How about we hit the floor," Steve said, handing me goggles and earplugs.

We hit the floor, walked right into the chorus of production. Steel mounting steel. The screech of cranking lathes. Sparks shot all around us. "The heat presses for the gasket valves get up to fourteen hundred," Steve said, pointing at a furnace-shaped machine where a woman pulled a lever up and down. Sweat flew off her bare arms as she yanked the lever, grabbed the valve with a set of clamps, then picked up another piece of metal from the pile. She yanked the lever down again.

Back in the office, Steve stared out his window at the parking lot. "Crazy to think this'll all be gone soon," he said. I was at his desk putting all the papers together. "My dad was a welder here," Steve said. "When I was a kid he used to take us to the company Christmas parties. They had a floor-to-ceiling tree, thing must've been fifty feet high, and we—hey, Mike?" Steve parted the blinds with two fingers. "What kind of car do you drive?"

The protest had split up into three groups: those who quit and now stood around smoking; those with their phones out, recording what was happening to my truck; what happened to my truck was the third group: maybe a dozen or so men—most armed with rocks, though one had a tire iron—beating the hell out of my dream vehicle. They punched and kicked and jumped on my truck's hood like this was something they'd been programmed to do.

That's why I took the train out to Worcester. The train was why everything else went to shit.

Inside the station, waiting near the Dunkin Donuts, I asked a woman if this was normal. She wore a suit, had her long red hair down, rolled on Chapstick. "The delay," I clarified. She took out her phone. I asked if she was familiar with trains—but she forgot I was there.

Rain when we left. I sat there on the train, alone, attending to my posture. The pain in my back got me thinking about Worcester Screws—all those products made from real American bones. It was better for the environment, for the patients, for the economy. Less and less space to bury. Cremations released vaporized mercury, dioxins. So what if all skeletons were put to use: hairbrushes, toothbrushes, dishware? Soda in bone bottles that decayed while sipped. Nothing to dispose. Replacing all the plastic on cars with bone. Stop chopping down trees, instead use bones for chairs, tables, shelves, coat racks. Then we'll be identical to the objects we use—but then, I worried, nothing would be sacred, because everything would be the same. An arm and a bottle. A screw and a skull.

"Are you okay?" This was asked by a woman now sitting next to me. I guess I was making a face. I apologized. She looked just like my first wife, this woman. We got to talking—she'd grown up in South Kingston, right near Sand Hill Cove Beach. I told her about Worcester Screws, about skeletal possibilities. She stood up, stretched, said she needed to check out the food car. She grabbed her suitcase from the overhead compartment before walking off.

The train rolled along.

A little later, unable to stop thinking about what a god-damn idiot I was, I decided to visit the food car. It was closed, the whole cabin was dark, but there was one pair talking.

Woman: There's almost no chance of surviving a plane crash.

Man: Train's still more expensive than the bus.

Woman: You're paying for two very different experiences.

Man: And still less efficient than a plane.

Woman: There are less direct flights now.

Man: And yet the question still stands.

Woman: Even if they're diesel powered.

Man: Excuse me? Hello there. Hi. Can I help you? Yes, you.

It took me a few seconds to realize the guy spoke to me, not her.

"Don't think so," I said.

The guy smiled, then turned toward the window. The woman tore a napkin up. I stood there for a bit, trying to think of something to say, something relevant, or for them to say something, relevant or not, but none of us spoke, and after a few seconds of listening to the soft hum from the car's overhead lights I walked off. Turned out an older couple had taken my row. Which was fine. Found another seat a few cars back beside a mother who had parked her son right in front of her. He was strapped into one of those electric wheelchairs, her son. I kept apologizing, but she scooted over and gave me the aisle spot. "It's not a big deal," she said. Took time to pass out, and when I woke up the mother was leaning forward with a napkin to wipe around her son's mouth. The kid had the biggest eyes I'd ever seen.

Kurt Ulrich, owner of Worcester Screws, wore khakis, boots. I stepped out of the station and found him holding a decorative sign with my name on it. "My daughter made it," Kurt said. I wanted the sign but figured it would be weird to ask.

"My wife is a nurse," Kurt said. "So I hear all about what forensics folks do with the bodies that get donated." We plowed along the freeway. Rain swirled all around us. The trees were bare and the foot or so of snow was melting. Kurt kept looking from the road to his phone. "One time some forensic scientist took my wife to see what he was working on. They go way outside of town. Douglass. Farm country. They come to this field and he's all, Here we are. There's nothing for miles. Naturally my wife gets to thinking she's about to become a billboard image. But then the forensic scientist points at the mulch, says they're studying how corpses decompose in different environments. That's what's all over the field. Not mulch, but corpses. And they're getting grants left and right for that sort of work. Makes no sense."

We rumbled across a bridge, right above the littered banks of a river, that dark dull water winding between the fields of stripped poplars, and then we passed houses, a brick school with every window boarded shut, and eventually turned down an unpaved road, tree branches smacked the windshield, and we parked out front of a building's remains, some jagged mass of re-bar and cement surrounded by a lopsided fence. A massive wheel of rust jutted above a partially crumbled wall.

I asked if this was Worcester Screws.

Kurt reached in the back seat and came back with an unopened bottle of bourbon. "I was hoping to get you in the factory before first shift showed up," he said. "We only have a first shift left now, so I guess I don't need to call them first shift. Anyway, they know things aren't going great, but they don't know I've already decided to shut the place down. Timing is everything. Once all the paperwork's done, once there's no way it can be reversed, that's when I'll tell them we're closing. Less chance for any drama." I took a sip of my drink and then, coughing, tried to say in a nice way that I still didn't understand what we were do-ing here. "I'm having one of my supervisors take all of first shift out to lunch, that way no one will see you and worry. When's your train out again?"

We drank and we talked. Rain on the roof filled the

silences. Listening to Kurt, I felt warm and sturdy, like I belonged somewhere, right here, up high in his seat-heated SUV, as if we were on neighboring thrones overlooking a just bombed land.

"It's about a lack of specialization," Kurt said. "We were what we did."

There was a bang from the rubble. Gulls flew off. My shoulders jumped a bit. A baggy-clothed guy stumbled out from behind a wall, and for some reason I worried he would run over and get in the car and stab us to death—especially once he hooked both hands in the fence—but then I noticed the steam rising from his crotch. He'd walked over to take a piss.

"Have you ever seen a corpse split open?," Kurt asked, turning from the door. We were in the stairwell of Worcester Screws. "I'll take you back to the cleanroom. It's like seeing an engine come apart."

Except we never made it to the cleanroom. We tripped through the doorway to find people waiting for us. Men and women, maybe twenty of them, all staring. The room was filled with benches and machines and had one crescent window, where in the gray light someone stood separate from the crowd, tapping a pry-bar against his leg.

"Looky here." Kurt was saying. "Back to work, let's go." He clapped his hands above his head.

"Who's that?," asked a guy with glasses.

"Michael." I stepped forward and offered a hand. "Kurt's Amish brother."

"Kurt doesn't have a brother."

I used that same hand to push some hair out of my eyes.

"Jimmy," Kurt called to the guy at the window.

"Our checks all bounce, then you want Jimmy to take us to lunch for no reason, then this guy shows up," someone in the crowd was saying. Their faces started to blur together.

"Jimmy, you want to explain this?," Kurt yelled.

"And you're still trying to lie," someone else said.

"Hey, hey." Kurt stepped toward the crowd and shoved somebody. "You know what I've done for you?" He pushed someone else. Then another person. The crowd shifted about. "Ungrateful. Disrespectful."

Someone pushed Kurt and sent him stumbling into the heat press. Then he lunged from the machine and swung into the crowd.

I stood there watching Kurt and the boys war it out. I wanted to do something, but I saw the guy at the window with the prybar run toward the fight. There came the sound of Kurt screaming. Everyone was huddled around him, kicking, punching. The prybar rose above everyone's heads and then disappeared.

I ran out of Worcester Screws and puked in a culvert, then grabbed a cab to the train station. Inside I stood very still, expecting something to happen, for someone to emerge from the crowd and tackle me to the ground. But nothing happened. I was free.

What followed was the greatest hour of my life. I knew that the disaster at Worcester Screws marked the transition, the point, when I willed all my failures to the past and started over. And what a sense of purpose in that hour! I strolled the aisles of the train seeing things as they truly were. I saw couples much younger than me asleep against each other, bodies knotted with hope. I saw an old guy hunched on the toilet—he forgot to lock the door—stare unflinchingly, unashamedly, when I walked in on him. Yes, I realized, I was what I did, and I had done wrong because I had done nothing, but that meant I could change—I could do otherwise, I could do better! Here I was, free on the train! Alone, therefore: free! And as I moved from car to car I decided that everything began in Worcester, that I would give my two weeks and begin a new life. I would write a play, I decided, a drama about the workers and the machines and the forces controlling the workers and machines.

When the cops met me in Merrimack, I prayed:

Dear Lord, fuck you for giving me a brain, and hands, and a heart.

And fuck you for giving other people brains, and hands, and hearts.

And for putting us within reach of each other.

Amen.

# CONTRAPASSO

Matilda Lin Berke

*I. Exile*

If you're in a dark wood, it's your fault.
You've cast off all your old skins for a new one,
but everybody knows just what you are.

Think for a moment on the things you've lost
and they'll consume you. You've never lost a thing!
(By you, I mean the guilty you: that's me.)

The more you get, the more you start to want.
The more you want, the farther down you go.
You're in it now. You'll get what you deserve.

Here lies the entrance to your underworld.
Here marks the margin of your wandering ways.
Here you will meet the faces that you've made—

*II. Amphitheater 1985*

In the Hollywood Forever Cemetery,
a peacock perched upon a granite slab:
abominably blue, distinctly blue

cyanotype over dead cinema.
I know just how I must have looked
to you: the beatific face of love,

when really, you loved her.
But you thought about me more—
the faulty mechanism

by which what happens
always seems to happen.

9

It was a teenage night,

as from a jewel box
mounted, emerald-cut—
you asked me if I'd see a band downtown.

Nothing is real until it really happens.
After the concert, high above the city,
you parked your car where no one else would go.

You slept that night. She stayed up thinking of you.
I stayed up thinking of her thinking of you—
the reel in motion.

Against the night, a shape projected
in a midnight film, guilt enfleshed,
stretched tight over its own protruding ribs—

they all KNEW WHAT I DID, THEY KNEW, THEY
KNEW—
in the headlights, the sorry truth emerged:
a half-alive coyote slunk away.

*III. Kandinsky & Klee*

In red, I launched a caustic triangle
across a canvas forested in green,
mortally wounding your Schiele *Self-Portrait*—

you laughed, you said you liked him more that way.
I know this now—you'd carved him out for days:
your favorite martyr, rendered faithfully.

I knew this then—
the face of your devotion.
It was easy to hurt you, then forget.

Dear friend, you were too quick to canonize,
sketching your patron saints, and watching me.
At turns I was Kandinsky, at turns Klee:

both sides, both halves, the answer to all things.
Just like you always told me—*form and feeling*,
dodging empty paint tubes I tossed aside,

and every time I cried, you wrote to me—
*Dear friend, you are yourself, not St. Sebastian*—
you bleeding heart. As if I'd ever suffered

from a surfeit of compassion—
well, that's love:
the savage gift of wanton oversight.

Now you know what I've done.
Oh, now it's out. My dear departed friend,
you drew me on the wrong side of the tree.

*IV. Camera Obscura*

The storm spooled down in silver on the lake,
expectant, soaking through your coat—and you,
a shadow on the foreground, begging me

to stay there with you, even for the moment—
how could I tell you no? You'd laid it out
in tableau, all right there, and just for me:

the picture, framed, the optical illusion
drawn up in perfect, or drawn close enough
if I squinted through the tight knit of the rain.

I think love is a nice word for attrition:
a slow erosion of the surface image.
I redrew it from inside, in sepia—

*la dolce vita* stitched up from a patchwork
pattern—vague ideas of real, sweet lives.
An image of us talking at a party:

two strangers trying to tell each other something
chrome-fixed that should have been left free and fleeting—
how could I have said no? It was right there.

A storm looks like a storm, a port a port,
a portrait made for two. The aspic portrait:
the face of love, a face we know too well.

*V. Sillage*

If everybody wants him, then I want him.
It's easy to be wanted in return. All I must do:
become a perfect replica. Observe

the honeybee, his routine transgressions
from flower to flower. He chooses carefully—
color, fragrance, feel, a distinct tone

of voice, all patterns set in early childhood—
forgone conclusions, the time-distant products
of random attars, chemical reactions—

nothing I can't fake, since basically
it's all just synthesis. I can do that—
make myself up to be the very same,

except for what? Except that it's not real.
I want what you have. You don't want what I have.
The absolute—and don't we all want that?

## VI. Beatrice

I'm looking for an object of devotion:
not love, but something. Something to observe.
This is an invitation: observe me further—

you see me now, that means I've made it out.
I'm writing from dry land, finally removed
and faint, the brush tail of a pleasant dream—

and when I wake, I don't need more than this,
the sole recourse of being so estranged—
you listen, then you tell me what I mean.

Nothing, it seems, feels like it's meant to feel.
I stayed up all night to see a meteor shower
alone—the dull and thickly plastered sky

tinselled with flaccid motions towards light.
I stared at one until it swelled and arced
in imitation of a falling star—

the difference: really seeing it, or not.
The distance between love and the other thing—
what does it matter, if you can believe it?


*My dearest friend, my dearest Beatrice—*

*I stayed up, half-believing in the sky,*
*believing in that chimerical light,*
*elusive, far-effulgent, quick retreat—*

*a secret held between that night and me.*
*The truth is less important than it seems.*
*The truth? A secret, hidden in between*

*the face you've made, the one you've waited for,*
*the sacred secret—what does it mean?*

*Yours,*

*from the dark further back, or farther on.*

# My Sponsor
Geoffrey Mak

In California, recovery is a booming business. While Alcoholics Anonymous was born in New York, it carries a distinctly homegrown iteration here, particularly in Los Angeles, which I've heard referred to as "the Mecca of recovery programs." It was, for me, the house at the end of the cul-de-sac. At my family's imploring, I decided I needed to get clean. At the outset, Alcoholics Anonymous offers itself as a book or a method, though its participants will stress that it is a community. Even in the earliest meetings I attended, I found it hard not to be impressed by the fellowship I observed. What I was looking for was grit and character, and I sensed as much in some of the men in these AA meetings—"the rooms" they call it—which I attended with the reluctance of a teenager enrolled in traffic school. (Thankfully, we still met masked and in person.) Some of these men I encountered were Crips members, ex-convicts, Mexican drug slingers, compulsive liars, privileged scions cut off from their trust funds, chemsex addicts, gay porn stars. The Big Book of Alcoholics Anonymous states: "We are people who normally would not mix. But there exists among us a fellowship, a friendliness, and an understanding which is indescribably wonderful." It was hard to short change this. Because this was L.A., I saw the occasional movie star or cable news pundit come through, though they were not the ones who showed up week after week. The dedicated regulars were the desperate and destitute, who at the end of the meeting, "prayed out" the Serenity Prayer and repeated, in unison, "It works if you work it, so work it, you're worth it."

"Goofy and archaic" is how one friend described his impression of AA, after I'd told him I started going. "Goofy" had its charms. But "archaic" retained a deeper allure. I bored easily with other programs, which were either New Age—inflected or had a cognitive behavioral therapy bent. AA was so incontrovertibly the real thing. Austere, and as thorough as a colonoscopy. I may not be off the mark in saying that the "Big Book" of Alcoholics Anonymous is the single most influential work of American wisdom literature of the last one hundred years.

Still, most actual meetings felt grating to me, like church. I rarely shared. Antisocial and made awkward by social distancing, I didn't approach others, and instead waited for people to approach me. The man who would become my sponsor was one of those people. Bald, with a mustache, he had on a checkered shirt with a red bandanna around his neck, and his beady eyes bore affectionate crow's feet. By way of introduction, he dropped, in our first conversation, that he was gay and Christian, which was apparent from the cross necklace resting on wisps of chest hair and his straight-fit leather pants, which were like the lederhosen all the fetish daddies wore in Berlin. Often, he showed up to meetings on his motorcycle, wearing a leather Harrington, and I could spot, from across the room, his idiosyncratic mustache that went from one of his sideburns, down along his jaw, up and across his upper lip, and then back down and up to the opposite ear.

Right when I saw him, I thought he looked like a daddy. In the rooms, he was held in high esteem because he worked at a rehab center out by the beach, dealing with day-zero addicts who were bouncing off walls. "Were you busy saving lives?" I'd say when I saw him. He came from the leather scene in New York and was old enough to have remembered when AIDS was called GRID. He'd been active in the gay motorcycle club and frequented after-hour sex clubs in East Village basements. But today, he had a scrubbed-clean image: a card-carrying Christian who listened to K-LOVE on the radio to destress. By the time I met him, he said, wincing, that he had been celibate for two years. His half-conscious abstinence—which made him alluringly untouchable—only called more attention to his repressed past, in which I imagined his low tenor issuing firm, affectless directions to a sub. I was probably in love with him.

Addicts are people for whom love comes easily. We ooze desire, barely able to conceal our battle against our forbidden drives. My sponsor secreted his sensitivity like sweat. He was constantly "falling" for people, often saying "I fell in love with her at that moment" or "I just love that kid" when describing clients

16

or coworkers. He cried openly in front of people, midconversation, in meetings; a touching habit he was unembarrassed by. He, of course, had his own history with addiction: had once frisked a pharmacy while working the night shift, had gotten so blackout drunk that he forgot having called his grandmother and telling her to "fuck off." He had demons—had been molested as a child, gang raped once—touchstones that were part of the "narrative" he shared regularly in AA. He reminded me that the haunt of relapse always beckoned, no matter how long you've been sober. He had been several years sober when he was invited to his own sponsee's house and stole all the pain medication from the bathroom medicine cabinet. This might have deterred me from asking him to be my sponsor, but rather, it made me trust him. He was transparent. Broken even, a word he personally disliked, saying it was an Old Testament word and "in Christ we aren't broken."

This was an unusual thing to hear in AA. While the program centers around the notion of "God," it's frequently euphemized as a "power greater than ourselves" of "our own understanding"; you never hear the name "Jesus" mentioned. ("The fastest way to clear a room," my sponsor joked). AA members refer to themselves as "fellows," not "Christians." But my sponsor was a full-on Christ-believing Christian. Sure, I had long-standing reservations with the evangelical church, but as for Christianity itself, I wanted so badly by this time what people in the rooms referred to as a "spiritual awakening" that I took in my sponsor's faith without any resistance. I wanted nothing short of ravishing passion, an abrupt and inner conflagration, that would push me toward a holiness so ecstatic it would feel treasonous.

What I found instead was duty and discipline, tedium and dailiness. As a sponsor, he was strict. For months, we talked seven days a week for one hour, at five p.m. on the hour. Each of the twelve steps was paired with a spiritual principle, from acceptance to integrity to brotherly love. Every step was accompanied by a set of assignments and readings, and I was expected to do them on time. We held certain maxims. God draws near to those who want Him enough. Where faith lacks, willingness suffices. My sponsor had rules: No self-pity or complaining of any kind.

No "past-dwelling" or "future-tripping," as both distracted from the present moment, which is all we have: "This is a day-by-day program." He barred me from using certain words, such as "drama" and "trigger" because they reeked of "unmanageability." If he sensed I was trying to protect or assert my "EGO"—his (goofy) acronym for "Easing God Out"—he would interrupt me, mid-sentence: "Excuse me, but I'm going to have to stop you for a second."

He was firm but polite, gentlemanly in his speech. He said "freaking" instead of "fucking." Often, he punctuated his sentences with "my friend," as in: "That, my friend, is the difference between emotionalism and true religious feeling." He was one to be wary of emotionalism: His chief vice was wrath, he said, which always threatened to consume him. I, too, knew it was a constant threat, and was careful to avoid it. Sometimes I suspected my flighty attention span irritated him. Whenever he made a point I was to focus on, he'd pause for several seconds until I said "Yes" or "Uh-huh" to show that I was tuned in. I dreaded that he would ask me to repeat what he'd just said (as he sometimes did), and I would be unable to answer because I had been zoning out.

I was afraid he could read my mind, quite literally in some respects. I often joked about his "psychic powers," because he used to be a psychic, which meant that when I told him that, in psychosis, I had entered other and potentially mystic realities, he remained as unfazed as leather. He said he'd attended a "psychic school" that trained some young psychics to go on to work for the police department or the FBI. They were given tests, such as being shown a spread of facedown cards and asked to flip over the queen. More often than was considered normal, my sponsor would turn over the queen. For a bit in his twenties, he worked as a professional psychic. Once, he scared a woman out of the room by calling her by a name only her dead grandfather used to say. Another time, he was a substitute teacher for a class, and a kid saw his pack of tarot cards peeking out of his bag from the floor. He begged for a reading, so my sponsor consented, performing one over lunch break. But "because once you turn yourself on, you can't really turn yourself off," he told the kid that his parents were making a difficult decision that would alter the course of his life. At that, he burst into tears, and ran to the principal's office. As it happened, his parents were getting a divorce. My sponsor was fired.

Which is to say that, sometimes, he could be unprofessional. In our early phone calls, he complained to me about how difficult or inept his other two sponsees were. They were unable to carry out simple assignments and they tended to catastrophize (the worst thing). These disclosures never felt entirely appropriate, though a part of me wanted to hear about how poorly the other two were because it meant I was the favorite. Occasionally, I would offer an easy aphorism about my readings in the Big Book—"Resentment is a desire for vigilante justice" or "Only innocence reserves the right to condemn"—and he'd say, "You're so good" with a smile. It made me feel dirty because of how much I enjoyed hearing it. "You have the gift of energy," he said, and I could hear his voice go buoyant on the phone. Some days, our calls went for an hour and a half, two. "I quote you to people," he'd say.

I was flattered, even if I was wary that our relationship was barreling forward to a point where I wasn't always sure when or how to pump the brakes. He would text me artifacts from his past which he'd "never sent any sponsee before," like a wedding picture with his ex-husband in New York or recordings of him singing Christian songs to the karaoke machine in his garage.

What exactly was going on here? I felt overwhelmed by intimacy. Privately, it triggered an identity crisis. I hated acting like a teacher's pet. To recuperate some critical agency, I would bicker with him if I found him tedious or clichéd. But he really did make me feel as if I'd been pitched back to childhood Sunday School. My sponsor required that I memorize certain prayers, and pray every morning bedside, on my knees. Later in our phone calls, he would ask, "Did you pray today?" Every time I said yes I felt like I was lying, even if I wasn't. As "service," he required that I do two chores in my parents' house every day, and text him, without fail, which chores I did. "The text is as important as the chore itself," he said. Later, I was to text him answers to

19

three daily questions: What I'd done well, what I could have done better, and who I'd helped that day. This was not, I concluded, a program for adults.

I fantasized about quitting, but never did. Eventually we went from daily calls to just four a week, but even then, the phone calls tended to blur. During some calls, I would lie on my bedroom floor, with the phone resting on the side of my face and an eye on my watch, punctuating the conversation with my yeses and uh-huhs. He would say, "You get me?" and I would say, "Yes." And if he suspected my mind was drifting, he would say, in an insinuating tone, "Do you?" This would both enrage me and flood me with guilt. Why did I always need to affirm him?

Though he was often the one affirming me, perhaps to the point where I felt I was being love bombed. "I'm in awe of you," he'd say about my insight. "My willing student," he said. "My friend." It made him giddy to get my calls unannounced. I could hear it in his voice. His earnest affection melted me. I collapsed into hysterical tears by myself one morning because I felt nobody in my life loved me as much as my sponsor. I was a drug addict, and he made me feel like the philosopher king. He was the first to tell me he loved me, and I could not get myself to repeat the phrase. "I have so much love for you, and I think it's mutual," he said, to which all I could muster was, "It is."

But, of course, I loved him, quickly and early. I wanted to give him the world.

I fashioned him in my mind as a lowly apostle, someone between Paul raving in chains and John the Baptist feeding on locusts and honey. My sponsor lived humbly, slept in a shared room in a sober living household, and worked just over minimum wage. Finances dogged him, medical bills piled. His superiors were always dangling promotions that never materialized. I tried to motivate him to apply for higher-paying jobs, but it was like pulling teeth. He didn't want to leave the addicts who adored him because he genuinely enjoyed them. He dignified them by considering them preferable company, like Christ did to prostitutes and tax collectors. "It's never draining," he said of the work, which otherwise had a staggeringly high turnover. "I'm where

I'm supposed to be." I looked at my own life and found it stupid and wasteful: all the designer clothes I never ended up wearing. Blessed are the poor in spirit, for theirs is the kingdom of heaven.

His lifestyle was not a rebuke to mine, but it always felt like it. The things that excited me—publishing in an international newspaper or getting a fan letter in my inbox from a fashion designer I admired—never captivated him. He extended to me the disinterested warmth of a father regarding his son's grade school marks. What overjoyed him was when I was late to a phone call once because I had lost track of time while praying. And so I began tailoring my attention. Out of habit, around him I clipped my emotions about trivial things, making sure not to feel anything too strongly, at the risk of being "dramatic." His masculine posturing could irritate me—for instance, when a bike accident on the freeway caused a hairline fracture in his ankle, he relayed this information to me like he'd gotten a migraine—and if I expressed shock or worry that he deemed too maternal, I would detect a hint of annoyance in his voice, and so I always backed off.

Yet his response recurred in my mind throughout my day like a rare blessing—"You're being dramatic"—as I complained to myself during the insulting repetitions of organizing cups to fit into the cabinet, the inanity of fitness, scouring the internet for new dinner recipes to make in my parents' overburdened kitchen. I lived for the dramatic. But to complain about tedium was to fundamentally misunderstand the task of life. Accepting the essential plainness of the real was a safeguard against being swallowed up by the whirlpools of one's own aggrandizements.

Once, when I relayed to him something a close friend had confessed to me, something I found quite sad—"shame is the air I breathe"—my sponsor rolled his eyes and said, "That's so dramatic" and I burst out in laughter. I couldn't help myself. This laughter felt juicy. After all, shame is ridiculous. Only conceited people feel shame: It's performative and masturbatory. There is no other way to respond but to laugh. One has no need to be ashamed of "the wreckage of one's past." One can simply regard it with warm disinterest and move on.

21

Which is what my sponsor taught me—that sobriety was a practice in humility and self-possession.

Yet so much of the time on the phone with him, we could not stop laughing.

Eventually, I finished the twelve steps. Inventory, amends, all of it. In my memory, the first six months of sobriety had dragged, but I barely noticed the six months after.

When my sponsor "graduated" me, I asked him for one favor to send me off: Could he give me a tarot reading? "In the name of Christ," I joked. He laughed bearishly and offered me this one occult indulgence.

He did the three-card reading. The first card, which represents my past, was the Emperor. Power, leadership, worldliness. The second, which represented my present, was the Eight of Wands. Creativity, rapid change, energy.

But when he flipped the third, I started once I saw it: the Fool. It's the first card in the entire deck.

"What does that mean?" I asked of the card that was supposed to represent my future.

He smiled ironically. "To approach life like a child."

# The Return of Maximalism
Julia Kornberg

It has been *vox populi* for quite some time. Self sells.
Readers today are inundated with a series of literary narratives
focused on the experience of the writer. Sometimes, this is ex-
ercised to the point of exhaustion and tedium, like Karl Ove
Knausgaard's painful (albeit beautiful) account of the self in his
seven-volume work *My Struggle*. Sometimes, writers do so with
a slight inclination for self-parody, such as Mario Levrero's *The
Luminous Novel* or Julian Castro's *The Novelist*. And sometimes
this results in a kind of numb, sensitive femininity, which is the
case for Sheila Heti or, even, the Nobel-winning novelist Annie
Ernaux. The author is dead, Roland Barthes seemed to claim, and
went on to write *Roland Barthes by Roland Barthes*. Reality, from
then, is only tied to bare facts of one's own personal experience,
and the subjective self has increasingly become the sole mechanism by which writers seem to understand, and modestly fiction-
alize, the world.

Although this mode of writing might have been en-
hanced in the 20th century and the tragedies that it engendered–
thus making the *testimony* a powerful political tool that follows
tragedy – the way in which narratives of the self work nowadays
seems to be more accurately traced to the religious practice of
confession. In this customary tradition of Catholicism, congre-
gants and sinners would gather, one by one, in a sanctuary, and
carefully retell details of their wrongdoings to a compassionate
priest, who would guide them in penance and absolution. Confession is dialogic, individualizing, and focused on moral ambi-
guities–and so is autofiction: a more-often-than-not exhibition
of the writer's own wickedness: sexual, emotional, or physical.
Modern writers write reality, yes, but they do so in a secular attempt to release themselves from it. Call this redemption through
pornography.

It would, however, be disingenuous to embark on another
diatribe against autofiction (because, alas, there are too many).
Instead, it might be more productive to dwell on the consequenc-

es that this has for fiction and imagination more broadly – that is, the way in which this focus on the self atomizes, shatters and deliberately limits the possibilities of imagination and prose. For, even when their stories are not an open confession or a literary seppuku, writers will boil down their ambitions into literary minimalism, and their imaginations only to characters that resemble them very closely. Since the development of subjectivity, there seems to be nothing outside the self, and the minimal prose that conveys it.

Sally Rooney, an Irish Marxist who inherits the traditions of Joyce and Brecht, of *Ulysses* and *Muttercourage,* has perfected this strain of individual fiction with an ascetic approach. Her novels focus on middle-class, global individuals from industrialized nations, usually millennials tinged with an interest in arts and politics. In her fiction there is no world building, but rather a refraction thereof – an attempt at identifying and reconstructing the millennial experience, in all its naked *dasein.* The tragedy of Sally Rooney, however, is not that of the predictability of her characters, but that of a prose which mimics it: her style is minimalist and legible, digestible, and soft. There is no complicated syntax, only scattered attempts at poetry. Reading Rooney is the cognitive equivalent of tap water: one leaves the book without the sense of having made the effort to read a book, with all the concentration and imaginative quality that it requires, but with the satisfaction of having read a book, regardless.

There is, then, simple politics followed by a simpler prose, and even simpler psychology. See, for example, *Lost Children Archive,* by diplomatic heiress Valeria Luiselli, a novel on migrant children that wander through the border between Mexico and the United States. In the novel, Luiselli successfully imagines her own children as lost children in the desert, crafting a series of academic and archival tools that enable empathy while exercising a sophisticated form of literary blackface. For the narrator, the migrant crisis is a powerful, political tool, a metaphor for her family's own state of disruption. The novel, originally written in English, and penned during the Trump era, is isomorphic with the flatness of American liberal political discourse, a boring elegy for the Obama era.

Autofiction mixed with party politics seems, then, to be the name of the game. Take, additionally, Lauren Oyler's hit novel *Fake Accounts*, about a woman whose boyfriend tragically dies and who, she discovers, was a secret online reactionary. Oyler, who worked directly for Obama's speechwriter, crafts a prose that attempts to hit all the nerves of millennial femininity – from her childless, empowered sensitivity to an opening sequence on climate change followed by a detailed account of all the steps on her skincare regimen. The novel, which reads sometimes as a laudatory epic of 30-something women, reveals to us progressively what the democratic party has been suggesting all along: that all white males are, secretly, White Supremacists. CNN couldn't have said it better, and Lauren Oyler says it with prose to make ChatGPT proud.

*

What happens when mainstream literature is so carefully lobotomized, so mimetically and uncritically in touch with the present moment to the point of exercising propaganda instead of literature? Where does fiction go when it wants to escape an algorithm that so carefully and simply tries to resemble reality? The consequence, as it may happen, is that the pendulum could swing back: among a myriad of narratives that seem imagined by an algorithm (located at the heart of the Pentagon), a simmering response might be emerging, wherein the most contrarian position to take might be to devote oneself fully, and expressively, to fiction and prose – and to do so, indeed, to the last possible consequences. Queue the weirdos, the recluse writers, the monomaniacal fictions, and ambition to the point of delirium.

Maximalist aesthetics repudiate simplicity, offer complexity and demand tyrannical attention, forcing the reader both to strain to understand as well as to be comfortable with what they don't know. They are intrinsically polysemic, sometimes defiantly lysergic, and deliberately maniacal. Maximalism requires effort and takes from their readers the same kind of attention that is necessary for prayer. Politically, its underlying ideology becomes irrelevant: all is deemed to prose, and politics are only as complicated as style. Saturated by the algorithm that creates best-selling books and DNC-approved fiction, fiction will inevitably turn to maximalism.

If the pendulum swings back and forth, Maximalism can be thought of as a traditional response to ascetic aesthetics. The genealogy might be sparse but ominous, hard to point out except by paranoia. Did it begin with Laurence Sterne's *Life and Opinions of Tristram Shandy, Gentleman*, which derided the superficial promise of total representation promised by the professionalizing, bourgeois author even as he was being created? Was it with *El Ingenioso Hidalgo Don Quijote de la Mancha*, when the desire of a new form for literature was overlapped with the exhaustion of the chivalric romance, giving birth to the most expressive, complicated, and creative form of parody? Or with Herman Melville's *Moby Dick*, who would latch onto his experiences of whaling to narrate the sea as if it was the New, New Testament? Was it with the New Testament, or the Old one?

In the 21st century, Maximalism might be derived both from high-brow modernist or post-modernist experiences of writing (say, a William Gaddis or a Thomas Pynchon, a W.G. Sebald or a T.S. Eliot) and, perhaps more importantly, from pulp fiction or weird fiction, with all its cheap and naïve calls for imagination. If the self is, increasingly, the only point of view which writers may allow themselves to inflict, if we have reached such a phenomenological point of malnourishment that a deep navel-gazing might be the only form of truth, Maximalism dynamites these singular perspectives and rejoices, more often than not, in the beauty of its rubble.

Three, recent books from Latin America and the U.S. seem to indulge in what we can call a Maximalist-gore aesthetic: Maximiliano Barrientos' untranslated *Miles de Ojos* ("A Thousand Eyes"), Ottessa Moshfegh's *Lapvona* and Missouri Williams' *The Doloriad*. The pages of all of these are covered with blood and carnage, with dismembered bodies and human secretions, with a detailed, Cronenberg-like eroticism. A sense of apocalypse follows all of these experiments: in a post-epidemic, warmongering world, these novels seem to suggest that this is just the experience of contemporary life, transposed and exaggerated into a virulent, crowded aesthetic. *Miles de Ojos*, by the Bolivian Barrientos, combines blood-thirsty black metal fans with portals opening in the middle of the sky, transporting characters through different dimensions. In it, pulp fiction is mixed with car crashes, motorized lingo, and Third World biker culture. *The Doloriad*, on the other hand, is perhaps even more devoted to this gore pour the gore, creating a lopsided world in which surviving humans dedicate themselves to surveillance, incest and to inflicting pain on each other. It doesn't have a narrative, really: just the dwelling, powerful gesture of its aesthetic force. *Lapvona*, perhaps the most reviewed and despised of this trio, is a historical fiction that takes place in a homonym European village, perhaps somewhere in Croatia, where Moshfegh's ancestors are from. Exercising her customary interest for all things abject – but taking it, this time, as far as possible from the self – Moshfegh created, with *Lapvona*, a seemingly unmarked territory where famine, agony, idiocy and evil take place. Although characters are often one-dimensional, and prose tends to falter, there is something in Moshfegh's attempt at total abjection in historical fiction to be celebrated. All in all, Mosfhegh, Williams and Barrientos write about places that they don't necessarily know, worlds that seem far from ours, and therefore advocate expressively for the craft of imagination. In their stylistic mishaps and geographical clumsiness, in their Maximalist projects and totalitarian theories over the world that they create, the value of all these novels is a contemporary rarity: ambition.

What do we do, then, when everything has been said, when frontiers of the avant-garde have been crossed, when all things have seemingly been obliterated, only to be invented again? Historical Maximalism, in this case, might be another possible end of this spectrum. Perhaps influenced by the postmodern mixing of non-fiction and fiction which granted the Nobel prize to historian Aleksandr Solzhenitsyn, or by the constant availability of encyclopedic knowledge doted upon us by the Internet, the Historical-Maximalist novel aims at creating a narrative fiction using real events from the past, digging them up as an archeologist would and then twisting their corners to fit into fiction. Historical fiction might even take a stab at autofiction, only insofar as it presents the figure of the author of a scribe, a sort of amanuensis of world history: if the author is present, then, he only is so as a reader, a vehicle upon which story attaches itself, to be molded and folded and worn.

W.G. Sebald's *Rings of Saturn*, whose diarist approach isn't much more than an excuse to revise everything from the history of colonialism to the silk road in 19th century China, sets perhaps the most valuable precedent for this. His novels, all of which are narrated from a melancholic first-person singular, circle around deeply dark subjects (say, English colonialism, say World War II and the Holocaust) and, labyrinthically, re-tell events surrounding it, building an oblique history that is composed of minor characters and events (a Chinese princess on the silk road, the worms that invented modern commerce). Contemporarily, Sebald created a school of his own, whose disciples go from the Croatian madness of Daša Drndić (whose *EEG* revises and re-imagines stories and characters living during the Balkan war) to the revered fiction of Olga Tokarczuk in *The Books of Jacob*, or the quiet sadness of literary men, such as the American Daniel Mendelsohn's *Three Rings* or the Mexican Daniel Saldaña París, who articulates history from the peripheries of Cuernavaca in *El baile y el incendio*.

However, no one has attempted to drive Sebald's technique as further as the Chilean writer Benjamín Labatut, whose *When We Cease to Understand the World* reads as an exquisite story of the chemical materials that created modern life, written from the fringes of the apocalypse. With a prose that has gleefully enraged scientists and historians alike, Labatut rewrites the arc of modern chemistry and physics – as well as the manias of the men behind them – to showcase a distorted image of progress, whose arch tends towards tragedy and massacre. Written in a Spanish that reads, almost, as a translation of Sebald by Michael

Hamburger (who famously transposed his dejected German friend into a pristine kind of English), Labatut slowly constructs a pyramid of rationality and war, where Zyklon B and Prussian blue serve as foundational stones for what will eventually become the tragedies that marked the 20th century. With the overlapping complexity of science and a textured, rarified style, Labatut's Maximalist approach, arrogant and unapologetically ambitious, offers many theories at once. The first one is metafictional and lies on the hypothesis that the basis of our modern world, i.e., the rational approach of the scientific method, creates the conditions of possibility for our Malthusian present and the massacre that it engenders. The second one is beyond his own literary accomplishments and, like *Lapvona*, is an urgency to writers and readers of the world: it suggests that there is more, in the gesture of its own ambition, to be achieved in reading and writing.

*

So, while publishers attempt to reproduce whatever formula has worked best (who is the next Sally Rooney? Who will write 2023's *Lost Children Archive*?) writers have assumed the task of imagining and creating literature anew, of transposing their ambitions into maniacal aesthetics. And perhaps, although this is nothing but naked speculation, there is something resembling exhaustion with contemporary narratives that allows those of subterfuge to boil with totalitarian, maximalist aesthetics. Perhaps this speculation is, then, a hopeful one: underlying it is the desire that, as a reader and a writer, there is more to be achieved, more to be read and written, further experiments to be made and new aesthetics to dispute, polemicize and create, as if in an infinite dialogue.

# Residential Rental Application

Sasha Starovoitov

<u>The Cast</u>

VINCENT: Born a stone's throw from the City, to a mother and a father and a house. Owner of the apartment, but only in verbal agreement, with no property to his name but a bit, but this does not bother him given the state of affairs in the world right now. Times are hard. Mid-height, hair of a dark complexion, in another life he would have gone by another name and perhaps one with more slick to it.

LADY: Myself as I am here. Mid-height, hair of a light complexion; in another life I would have gone by no other name and would be by Vincent's side, still, perhaps with a bit more slick to me, but not enough so as to lose my space.

STEPHANIE: Something unknown as of yet.

PLACE: The apartment, an apartment, in the City. It is not mine, but it is Vincent's and it is becoming ours, this is my plot: the arc of the apartment coming into my hands making me have a hand and foot in the door. Owning property is a slippery situation in the City and times are tight, I know it's not easy. So I'm here as a place-holder and that's a prized spot to have for someone in this economy in these times. I am the space.

TIME: Evening and then morning and also all other times. I am good with time. I know it well. But even though I know it, there's no denying—times are hard.

I used to come out when I wanted to but now I only come out when I am told.

Vincent comes home late. Stephanie, but she says call her Marie, *emphasis on -ie like MaRIE,* she says to me, comes home with him too, and I know they've met without me and I am hot but I just busy myself thinking because I have lots stored up in there for when the time comes, so I come to the room with the couch where they are all close, sliming up on each other I say—but Stephanie is eating his neck with her wet mouth and I cannot say anything because it's only Vincent who understands all without me even saying. When I think I'm understood but it is an ache to speak on un-understanding mouths like Stephanie's.

Vincent has little thought for the interruption that he has brought into the room, but it is his room after all, so I keep quiet and tight and I catch a mood that's better for new names. It is in Vincent's nature to forget that there is an understanding between us. It is up to me to remind him that it—the understanding—is understood and that we are happy like this.

I know Stephnie's name from Vincent's messages I pry from the phone every morning, pluck! Crouched next to the bed and I read names so our understanding stays understood: Stephanie in written word says *call me Marie, it's the name I use for work,* Vincent typing something that I would never say in response— he forgets himself sometimes and it's up to me to hold it all down here. So when she says this all to me, said walking in the door, I'm pretending like it's new, but I already know it all.

VINCENT: *Come sit.*

STEPHAN-MARIE:

Her voice is like sandpaper and it's getting long a rope curling around my throat she says

*Come siiiii-iiii-iiiit.*

The couch is full and I think where to put myself and Vincent, as if knowing, reaches out arm and hand and pulls me into him. Vincent is looking out of the window at nothing; he is calm and I am loving the curve of his nose against the noth-ing-black of the window, the flickering of candles I lit knowing they would come home in the mood to collapse like tangled

31

knots on this couch that is always sinking too deep.

I know how to set the mood. Candles are good for moods; so is a mouth, but be it silent.

He turns his head and we are looking at each other. I melt into Stephanie melting into Vincent; all three melting into each other. What's in my head right now? Lines of clothes and underwear I hung in the hallway because there is no drying machine and no washing machine and the bathtub is where I sit with my clothes and wash myself alongside cotton. I am clean and smell nice. There is a predictable physics to the motions of making something out of something (some say it's out of nothing and they'd be lying; there's never nothing when there's so much something to be had here). It is important to wash oneself well, this we all know, but do we practice it? Everything good comes from practice, this we all know too, but do we practice the practicing? Few have it in them, the foresight, to practice practicing and it is the very best who grew up knowing that practice makes not only perfect, but permanent and permanence is a rarity these days. These days, these days. I am bored of talking about this time and these days.

Vincent's hand is on my breast. Stephanie moans, but there are no hands on her, only Vincent's fingers lightly upon me and her hand upon me, and I glow, fly above all three bodies and slam into the ceiling to look down from my golden nest.

Cuckoos lay their eggs in the nests of other birds, tricking the bird into raising the false egg as their own. There is a buzz and I see little black dots circling around us.

Did I say it was the stillest day of summer yet? Mosquitos and gnats breed on still water and boy, was it a hot one and nothing could move a muscle it was just too hot! So we took to lying and Stephanie's leaking black beneath her eyes, her lips furry around edges like she's eaten too many popsicles and we're all wet. Hot skin on the couch makes me itch. When I was seven I took a bath after getting into the weeds and then my whole body was on fire. But we're just puddling now. A gnat flies into my eye and it weeps.

Two women weeping we are now.

VINCENT: *Lady, can you go close the window? These fucking flies are getting everywhere.*
STEPHAN-MARIE: *But if we close it, there won't be any breeze anymore.*
VINCENT: *Not like there's any coming in anyways. It's just hot air. And these candles aren't making it any better, Jesus Christ, why are they still lit? Lady, can you put them out? We're in a heat wave and you're lighting candles. A true romantic you are, trying to roast us all to death*
*THWACK!*
My breast is without his hand and he slams it against the wall. A smear of gnat on the wall now and I get up to pull the old window with all my weight, the wood swollen with waves of humidity and I hang on it to slam it closed like CHK! Stephanie jumps. Bloated walls are ours now. That's okay. We'll pay off the apartment and fix them right up, flowers on wallpaper but no one does that anymore, I'll read magazines and slip into the doctor's office to steal what's in.

Good. I blow the candles out. Stephanie coughs. It smells bad now in here, thanks a lot, why don't you ever think before you set the mood?
STEPHAN-MARIE: -- she's cooing, lips round. My mouth is too straight. My lips are two lines. When I open them they form a right angle at the cupid's bow cornered and there's a square in the middle of my face. Wah-wah-wah is all I say with cornered-lips-square-mouth. I come back to the couch and they pull apart this time, separating out their slug-selves, so I settle in between and sit like I'm at the bus stop, legs crossed and hands on knees. Good girl. I am waiting patiently! I want to eat Vincent. Wah-wah-wah. Corner-edged lips make for big bites.
VINCENT: *Ste-Marie, what'd you think of the crowd at the cafe tonight?*
STEPHAN-MARIE: *That place is just getting so annoying. You know, full of kids who think they get it. I miss when it was our place, like remember when we would go and sit in the corner and just look at everyone? That's how Lady came up to us, right Lady? Remember that?*

33

LADY: *Haha, yeah. That was such a fun night.*
LADY: *Does anybody want watermelon? I always have some when it's hot, it's like my favorite summer thing.*
STEPHAN-MARIE: *Oh what a good idea, Lady! I'd love some. Will you grab me a few slices?*
VINCENT: *When'd you have the time to go out and get watermelon? And where?*
LADY: *I just ran out to the store while you guys were out. They're marking up the watermelons because it's so hot and everybody wants some but I picked a half-one with a lot of seeds and brought it up to the cashier and pointed to them, like, there's so many seeds here, it's a bad one, I'm not buying it until you give it to me for less.*
VINCENT: *And did they?*
I am bored.
LADY: *Well, actually I just put it in my bag and walked out.*
VINCENT: *So you stole it?*
LADY: *I guess so.*
STEPHAN-MARIE: *That's like, what we should be doing anyways. Everything is so expensive nowadays, it's just crazy.*
And actually I am so bored I don't care, so I get up un-peeling and go to the kitchen. There's no lights and I don't turn them on. It's too hot now for light. I plunge my hand into the drawer for a knife and put my whole body into it into the watermelon and CRRRRRRAAAAACK! It splits into two. Then slices. I take a bite out of Stephanie's slice so there's only two points now. She won't even see it cause it's so dark now. Too bad! I put the watermelon on a plate and put on the voice and say here is watermelon, enjoy!
VINCENT: *Did you do anything else today Lady?*
LADY: *Oh, not really. Applied to a few jobs.*
I've been laying eggs in all the closet drawers but that's a secret for another day. I keep busy but they don't know that. I've got a nest on top of the refrigerator but it's not for prying eyes or minds. I brush my hair until half of it is gone and rip it out of the brush to braid it all back again and tuck it into secret places. Sometimes I shower two, three, four times a day. I'm there like

34

I'm on a schedule. Let's get moving, I yell at the showerhead. I'm in the business of secrets nowadays. There's just too much noise. Wah-wah-wah. Nobody can understand me when my mouth is shaped all wrong. What did I do today? None of your business! Everything is itching. Welts are rising on my arms and in the slippery pockets of my legs.

A job is too much for me to handle right now, but Vincent gets hung up on them; something to do, he thinks, unknowing about all that I am doing while he is out.

STEPHAN-MARIE: *It's so tough out there right now, like, I'm so glad I have a job right now. I just can't even imagine looking for one right now.*

Stephanie is a seller but also she's trying to make it big, but also she's done with the scene, but also she's just scoping things out, but also she's on the up-and-up, but also she's got a name, she's going somewhere, and most days she is out and about and then she sells. She sells and ships packages. Always the post office with her. I don't like the post office, too much paper-smell and too many corners. Stephanie is just figuring it out, she's just. She's at the clothing boutique and she's at rehearsals and she's never got enough money to pay the rent, but she's still in that studio that she's never at because she's here at Vincent's. And me? Well, I'm here too.

But I haven't said much about this City at all, have I? But it is unlike and like all cities really. There are many like Vincent living and saying silly things here and there and always leaving like they own it all so they can, but those of us who have nowhere to live—we've got to live in a place to make it un-leavable for the leavers. Liveable. Vincent is a man like other men in this City who enjoy a drink and work and also never, ever work. Vincent is always not working. But aren't we all? I am working on the place, not having had a job nor wanting a job and lying about all the jobs I'm looking for which is really just my job now, lying about all the jobs I'm looking for. And Stephanie is selling. That's barely work. She never breaks a sweat.

Outside of the City, there are outskirts and that's where men come in from. They can walk on sidewalks and some of us never had the time to learn how streets run up and down and side to side. The first days I moved here I actually never walked at all; I took to crawling on all fours because this way I could place one hand foot in front of the other and never look up at the great expanse of sky and all the buildings. I'd never seen so much blocked out and to not know the land, that was not something that I took to with ease at first during my first days in this City. There was some solace in dressing as a man in those days because it gave me two good feet to stand up on without the fear of stones upon my head or slipping out beneath my feet.

But it is when I walk with Vincent that I walk on my own two feet freely; in his arms that I am like a graceful girl again with airs above my head and I can smile out like a star. We don't walk much anymore together but that is because there is so much to be done here! There is a place to stake claim to. Space is hard to come by, haven't I mentioned? Some women have taken to sliding into the sewers and crawling out of men's sinks just to get a place to stay. But this is never easy. There is a stink and they've got to fix it somehow to be all peachy for the man to want to give her space.

At least I am not like Stephanie. She's a seller—there's a stink to that she'll never get out.

I'm here. That is a job in itself, being here, to make a place into a place where we want to be to spend time, these places are all vanishing here and there so I've taken to making places of my own. A job is too much for me to handle, but a home, that's good for the time being. And in a home there isn't any time anyways and that's what we all like. No days allowed, especially in the summer!

Vincent takes a triangle.

VINCENT: *I mean, it's just grotesque. The way we work, the way we live. The way we don't live at all anymore. A world made out of the unreal meant to feel hyperreal; condensed life into a matter of constant attention manipulation and infinite interruptions, stealing time from us in an endless simulacrum. Systems of control amplifying the simulacrum of freedom. It's a farce. The more freedom you're told you have,*

36

*the more choice, the less you truly possess.*

STEPHAN-MARIE: *Yeah, like, nothing really feels real anymore. Except this!*

Vincent is not eating the watermelon I cut.

VINCENT: *The collective, the love, the eros, there's no un derstanding left of what it meant to be one in relation to oth ers, one without being the only one, one without violence.*

Vincent is not eating the watermelon I cut.

VINCENT: *And actually, the loss of self does not mean the loss of the Self: the non-definite, primal core. But we've become too repulsed by the non-definite, the non-marketable, the unbranded Self that exists without entering into tacit agreements with structural modes of extracting*

Vincent is not eating.

*profit, the body that can work and now the mind that must work at rendering itself a coherent object. When in fact, inco herence is a treasure. A mode of rebellion long forgotten in this decadent*

Vincent.

*technocratic civilization. The interior becomes conflated with the efficient. Efficiency is death to the soul.*

Vincent is not eating the watermelon I cut. Stephanie is eating Vincent's neck again, getting it sticky with her watermel on mouth and Vincent is not eating the watermelon I cut. There would be no more words if he ate what I wanted him to eat. He is holding the triangle like a scepter. We're in a castle in the mid dle of the desert. There's a man riding his bike past our window and he's got a radio, the heat means everything is so loud but he's found space for more sound and finally, Vincent pauses to take a bite of the watermelon. I want tea. It's too hot for tea and I just sat down, wouldn't it be rude of me, but aren't I the host after all?

STEPHAN-MARIE: *Vincent, you should get an air conditioner.*

VINCENT: *My lease is almost up anyways, there's no point. I like this place, but I'm thinking of leaving the City. It's too parasitic. I don't have enough time for what I really want to be working on, like, it's all work but not my work, you know? I need to breathe. And besides, air conditioning would disrupt the space. Makes it unreal. We're meant to feel heat.*

STEPHAN-MARIE: *But it's impossible to do anything when I'm so hot.*

If I look at Vincent one more time not looking at me I'll be sick. There's bits of me all over this place, I'm molting and that sure does use up a lot of energy, man, it is exhausting and I get up again. I need a pick-me-up. And actually this heat is good, good for making everything settle. You can't move too much in the heat and sometimes we're all needing a break from it, now there's an excuse for us all except Stephanie said I need to get out of my studio, can I come to yours? Now we've got too much damn heat in this place. But in the kitchen I put water on the stove for tea and I don't ask anybody if they want any. I can take hot liquid in any heat, they can't, but for me it's just one-one and done in and out. I'm one with it, I'm down. Have I mentioned that? That's why I'm here. I'm down the most down I'm co-oo-ol in this heat, baby, Lady keeping it cool and always down. Yeah!

I'm dancing in front of the kettle thinking about how down I am. They can't say anything anymore. I'm down.

VINCENT: *Lady, are you seriously boiling something right now?*

LADY: *Yeah.*

VINCENT: *Why would you want to boil something right now? The stove is heating everything up even more, Jesus Christ.*

LADY: *I wanted some tea.*

STEPHAN-MARIE: *Iced tea would be so good right now.*

LADY: *There's no ice.*

STEPHAN-MARE: *Vincent, you don't even have ice trays?*

VINCENT: *Never got around to it. Don't see the point. Not like I'm staying anyways.*

I want ice trays and big glasses round like orbs and tall thin ones, flutes they're called, and a snow cone machine and a salad spinner and a house that pumps and beats with the sound of dancing cause we're all drinking ice-cold drinks in the summer heat and there's music, Vincent playing the guitar and I'm all like da-da-da we're harmonizing without even speaking, it's like magic all of our guests whisper in between licks-bites of cherry-blue-raspberry snow cones. I grew up around a lot of plastic. Wah-da-wah-da. I am waiting for the water to boil still dancing still making my own music,

LADY: *Vincent, can you put some music on?*

VINCENT: *Marie, can you put on some music? The speakers are over there.*

STEPHANIE: *Sure, what do you guys want?*

VINCENT: *Lady, you in the mood for anything in particular?*

LADY: *Oh, I don't know. Something upbeat? I have a lot of energy all of a sudden.*

Water is boiling. I take my tea and Stephanie isn't on the couch but now I am, I'm here. Sometimes I am a daughter but at other times I run this show, I put my legs on Vincent and I know what I'm doing. Stephanie was here before I was but I'm all over this place. My finger-nails are in the bathtub and my fingers, sometimes I leave them on the sink just to make a statement. I'm not stupid. I know what's going on.

There's a sound— Stephanie's put something on. All we do is put things on. I don't know it.

But here's the trick: I'm the best at pretending. Stephanie thinks it's her because she's a seller and sellers sure do know how to sell a smile but I know she can't find the beat for shit. But I can and I see it now: and I do it. There's been hours of rehearsal all leading up to this moment. I can only stomach so much mirror time but a pair of man-made eyes are exactly what I need to get my feet moving all smooth, my body swaying, hips and body and people always say they're getting lost in music but me, I'm not lost, I'm not found, I'm just moving. It's not too hard. Cleaning is like this too.

Vincent can't do either, he's on the couch, he has the lease and I do feel like just another plastic thing sometimes bought off of the television like my grandmother used to, phoning in, making her voice all up-glazed saying "yes" a lot.

39

My welts are going away now that I'm moving the wind. I make a cold breeze and the itch subsides. It is terrible to feel an urge. My stomach is always growling. I'm always needing a glass of something and always, always thinking of something else. I step out of my skin now. Stephanie is tapping her foot, she's wanting to dance and without my skin I think I can handle the company of another on the dance floor so I reach out a hand. Me? Yes, you. But you've got to take that off. We say this to each other and Vincent, he's looking like a fish. Wah-wah-ha-ha!

I went to a dance party once except I've got two feet that don't know how to move right so they just move left and I ended up against the wall all on my own, I felt like I was a strange man so I pretended to undress everyone with my eyes and did I see some things while I was a man! I tried to think in vectors not planes. But that was still too hard so I cut it down to just lines. And always only one at a time. All the women on the dance floor lost their faces like a receipt at the bottom of a purse and all the men grew hair on their chests and when I looked down I saw that my own chest had become all wolf-ish like a famous actor's. I thought I could be a handsome man. But then a girl pulled me back into the crowd, took my hands, showed me how to move my feet from side to side so that's how I'm showing Stephanie now like shuffle-1-2-3-shuffle-4-5-6-and-sli-i-de. There's no name for the dance, it doesn't need one, but she's gotta step out of her skin too if we're going to find our rhythm, she's got to notice how mine's left behind on that couch welded into the fabric still itching. I'm not anything as I'm dancing now, no vectors or lines or planes in my head, I'm not looking at others anymore, not a man anymore, never was really just trying it on for size. I am so hot!

And I do know a good way to break up the atmosphere here, to take a bit with me and slice it up thick. Vincent has his tea, he's comfortable, but us girls, we can cut the tension like no other. That's what us girls have to do. When I'm a man on the dance floor I can say what is and isn't, but as a girl, all I can get is a we and we know who isn't us, it's him, that's how I get them into my league. We're on the same team, girl.

LADY: *Stephanie, do you want a cigarette?*

MARIE: *Oh, I don't really…*
LADY: *I have like, half a spliff in my purse.*
VINCENT: *I can't fathom why you would ever elect to so willingly poison your body like that.*
LADY: *Well, I'm gonna step out. You can join if you'd like.*
MARIE: *I'll come. Hold up, let me just grab my jacket.*

A man gave me a cigarette a long time ago and I have hidden it in the small divot behind my ear just for this very moment, knowing I need to be a girl with other girls. It's easy to be a man and it's much harder to be a girl, especially with other girls who have good eyes and good noses and good ears and good teeth to tell when things turn sour. Teeth ache when biting into cold but also, more importantly, when things turn sour, that's when teeth ache the most— any girls ill tell you that. It's hot but smoke makes summer. Always grab a deal, nothing's free unless you make it so. I'm always one, two, three, four hundred steps ahead, especially when it comes to Vincent. He's allowed to be in the moment, but us girls? Never. I pack a spare pair in my bag, I'm brushing my teeth over the train tracks before stepping on looking like the freshest flower.

Me in Vincent's slippers-- I know what I'm doing-- and we go out. Air is big in me and I'm big again.

LADY: *You know he's a piece of shit, right?*
MARIE: *What?*
LADY: *Vincent, you know. He has, like, so many other girls coming through here.*
MARIE: *Oh yeah.*
LADY: *You didn't know?*
MARIE: *Well, yeah. He told me you like, practically live here. But I have my own thing I guess. It doesn't bother me.*
LADY: *That he's sleeping with so many other people? You don't get jealous?*
MARIE: *No. Do you?*
LADY: *No.*
STEPHAN-MARIE:
LADY:
STEPHANIE:

41

I go to sleep with a toothache.

In the morning I am up first. I am always up first. The birds and I speak through the window. How was your night, how was yours, bad, good, I'm crushing glass into the coffee because Stephanie's bag is on the couch, there's me in the boiling water running red but I'll start all over again until it runs clear and I can say good morning with a good smile for the lovebirds. How was your night? How was your night? I practice. How was your night?

LADY: *How was your night?*

LADY, with a smile: How was your night?

Enter LADY as STEPHANIE as MARIE.

MARIE: *How was your night?*

MARIE [*as LADY in disguise*] *wakes up, scented sweet.*

MARIE: *Hello, my love. Do you love me? Oh, I adore you. Oh, how we love each other!*

VINCENT [*as LADY as VINCENT [as VINCENT having just woken up*]]: [*Aside*]: *Oh Lady, you smell so sweet right now— how did you sleep, my love?*

LADY [*as LADY as MARIE having just woken up next to LADY as VINCENT having just woken up next to LADY as MARIE*]: *I slept so sweetly, my love, and waking up in your arms is like rising into yet another dream.*

Dishes left in the sink and on the couch and everywhere are mine for scrubbing now, I am one of many women scrubbing but it's a mistake to think I think I don't want this. There's my nest and there's bits of me everywhere and this scrubbing is how I make sure I'm woven in, I'm a tapestry laid down beneath the floorboards growing in beneath Stephanie and Vincent's feet when they leap upon me like two love-birds. I am I am I am I am I am. Wet water dripping from my dish-washing makes for moldy corners. I do my best to keep clean though. If not for me there'd be dishes in a pile, nothing but stink.

We women do like to weave, don't we? And weep?

And I'm no stranger to that, sure. I have and had a mother, maybe a few sisters or none at all, but definitely, I've sat around in a circle weaving. And oh what I've weaved with my girls! We weave about everything; there's this boy and that boy and this man and that man but I know I have something locked up. I've woven myself into my man. I've woven myself into my man's home. Dream big, girls.

Stephanie comes out and she's got on her underwear.

STEPHANIE: *Oh! Sorry. Didn't know you were out here.*

LADY: *Haha, yeah, I get up early. The light woke me up.*

STEPHANIE: *Did you sleep on the couch?*

I slept on the floor in the other room. The bed I have made too comfortable for guests but not comfortable for my itchy legs and hands, sleep tight, but all I hear is Stephanie's breathing in my bed that I stretch sheets onto silent, behind the scenes, Vincent saying, these are so soft, and he doesn't know I pour vinegar into the bathtub when I'm scrubbing sheets to make them so. I'm digging the holes into the walls, he'll know and notice and call me to say you've made me so soft, come back! All I want is to hear a boy beg sometimes. So I sleep on the floor when my bed's too busy, because that other bed, it's for guests.

LADY: *Oh, we have a bed for guests in the other room.*

STEPHANIE: *Nice.*

LADY: *Do you want coffee?*

STEPHANIE: *I actually should get going— I have so much to do today, I can't believe I slept in. I'll just grab my things and head out, I think.*

I make coffee. I pour. My hands feel good staying busy to bring more good around. Soon I will have a child I think! I am good at keeping secrets, haven't I mentioned? Secrets do well in the belly down low. Haven't I mentioned I'm the best at pretending?

I am.

The door shuts, Stephanie out now.

But I'm good at being me too, that's what's most important. Be me be I I am, I am I am. I am!

Vincent is stirring I hear in the other room so I go, I like to be the morning sun! I am the morning sun! I read in spare hours, especially when I'm lying beneath and within and between things because that makes for an idle mind and nobody likes the

43

hum of spare rooms. And I know what they say; I know to be the first thing. In the night I pour syrup into his ears and seal it with a kiss. Mwah! Remember me, remember. Remember, we have an understanding. I leave favors. A kiss upon a handkerchief is what's best but that's not now so sweets in ears it is for me and I know the recipe. I know lots, knowing is what I'm actually best at— weaving comes from knowing and cleaning comes from knowing and growing comes from knowing so I know, I know and that's what makes me best for here. But I've just got to make sure Vincent knows that and he's no good at knowing at all.

Lots of -ing in being ready being knowing, I get tired of all the inginigning I do around here but it's just how it is, there's no birds, and that's just the way it is, and I'm digging holes into the corners and building nests in the closet and that's just the way it is.

Here is what I am: ingining, and inside of there, isn't there an ininin? In the closet in the room in the apartment in the house, somewhere, and I'll be -inging all that I know, to be me is to be in action and inside because this is how I make sure I have a spot for the future by Vincent's side. Stephanie makes a mistake by leaving here, she'll be forgotten if I scrub away at the spot enough. Scrubbing spots drives one mad but not me; I've mentioned, yes, that I have learned how to be in a place for just long enough so that I am.

# Excerpt from the play *"Galatea 2.0"*
Sophie Dushko

*silence.*
*he looks up from the phone, meets her eyes, sees her.*
*a moment of connection—she breaks it.*

**eliza:** sorry, that was
    weird.
    anyway.                **henry:** no, uh--
    uh.
    tell me about you.

**henry:** i…

**eliza:** what do you do?
    for work?

**henry:** me?
    i, uh, well,
    tech.
    stuff.

**eliza:** tech.
    stuff.

**henry:** right.

**eliza:** what kind of
    tech.
    stuff?

**henry:** oh.
    boring stuff.
    nothing you'd / be --

**eliza:** is it, like,

coding?

**henry:** oh.
    yeah, yeah.
    mostly.

**eliza:** huh.
    my dad's always on me about coding.
    learning to…
    "it's the way of the future"
    "good skill to have"
    you know, for the "job market".
    or whatever.
    "in 10 years
    even 6 year old kids
    will know how to code"
    like they'll learn it in first grade
    or something.

    *she laughs.*

**henry:** well, actually/ they —

**eliza:** sorry.
    shit.
    i sound like i'm --
    i think it's
    cool
    that you "code".
    "mostly. "

**henry:** uh, thanks.

    *silence.*
    *she blows on her tea. sips.*
    *realizes it's cooled down and sips again.*

**henry:** so, what do you do?

*she looks at him.*

**henry:** oh.
    fuck, i'm sorry.

**eliza:** it's ok.
    i like what i do.

**henry:** good.
    that's good.

*she smiles.*
*silence.*
*she takes another sip of tea.*
*it's awkward.*
*he proceeds with caution:*

**henry:** have you ever --
    uh met—or --
    seen one?
    a real one?

**eliza:** a real...?

**henry:** oh, um, a —
    doll.
    a love doll.
    like from the photos?

**eliza:** oh! sure.
    i mean, i went on some websites?
    of companies that
    like a1 and stuff?
    realdoll?
    is that what you--?

47

**henry:** right.
     that's--

**eliza:** yeah.
     crazy.
     they're, uh…
     those things are
     really fucking expensive.

     *she laughs, he kind of joins her.*

**henry:** i…
     have one.

     *silence.*

**eliza:** oh.

     *silence. he's working up the courage to:*

**henry:** i could --
     introduce you.

**eliza:** oh.

**henry:** only if you / want —

**eliza:** right.

**henry:** what?

**eliza:** i just said right.
     but…
     uh.
     yeah.
     yeah.

you can
introduce me.

*she smiles. he smiles.*

henry: o/k--

*eliza's phone vibrates in henry's hands.*

eliza: shit, sorry.

> *she takes the phone from him,*
> *looks at the screen,*
> *declines the call and puts it in her bag:*
> *she's committed to being here.*
> *she looks at him expectantly.*

eliza: all yours.

henry: uh ok.
give me a minute.

eliza: sure.

henry: uh…
actually.
could you wait in the kitchen?
while i…

eliza: oh, yeah, sure.

henry: ok.
thanks.
i'll come get you
when she's…

eliza: ready?

**henry**: right.
      yeah, ready.

*she starts to go, taking her mug.*
*she points to his like "are you done?"*

**henry**: uh, yeah,
       thanks.

*she picks up the other mug and heads to the kitchen,*
*looking back over her shoulder at **henry** who is visibly anxious,*
*he paces for a moment, trying to calm himself down, before leaving*
*through the other door, presumably to the bedroom. the lights dim but*
*do not fully darken.*

*seamlessly, upon **henry's** exit,*
***mrs. pat** appears in her spot, without her dog.*

# The Nothing Economy
Micah Cash

*"What would one of our ancestors have said upon seeing these boulevards lit as brightly as by the sun, these thousand carriages circulating noiselessly on the silent asphalt of the streets, these stores as sumptuous as palaces, from which the light spread in brilliant patches, these avenues as broad as squares, these squares as wide as plains, these glittering trains, which seemed to furrow the air with fantastic speed?"*

Jules Verne, Paris in the Twentieth Century

In a sixty second spot that aired during the 2022 NBA playoffs, a woman in a sequin dress dances at a wedding reception. "You know why people are always looking at their phones?," she asks to the camera. "They're banking with Bank of America." Cut to various guests at the wedding, grinning over their handheld screens. Cousin Jimmy's girlfriend just caught the bouquet, "so he's checking in on that ring fund." The photographer is dreaming of his own yoga studio, pressing a big blue button that reads "Start a Business." Phil forgot a gift, so he's wiring the happy couple $150. The parents of both the bride and the groom are also featured; even during your child's wedding, "you just can't stop banking." Finally, the tagline: "what would you like the power to do?"

From 1978 to 2015, inflation-adjusted purchasing power (or "real income") for the bottom half of Americans decreased by 1 percent; for the richest one percent, real income nearly tripled.[1] While it's indisputable that something is deeply broken, the culprit depends on who you ask. Keynesians blame austerity and Hayekians blame entitlements; leftists blame monopoly power and union-busting and the right blames woke corporations and the snowflake laptop class they employ. Most likely, the tech-

---

1    Facundo Alvaredo, Lucas Chancel, Thomas Piketty, et al., "Global Inequality Dynamics: New Findings From WID.world", *NBER Working Paper* 23119, 2017.

no-capitalist economy of rich democracies is far too complex for any grand unifying theory, but macroeconomists must at least pretend to understand the world, and from globalization to manufacturing decline to the magic wand of innovation, theories abound.

In his book *Keystroke Capitalism* (Verso Books, 2022), philosopher-turned-economic-sociologist Aaron Sahr proposes a new candidate: the unchecked ability of private banks to issue credit, creating money from nothing. In Sahr's telling, the history of banking in the West is an ever-increasing separation between banks' lending privileges and their actual currency reserves. Sometime between the 13th and 15th centuries, "money changers" began the practice of issuing paper receipts like IOUs to replace cumbersome gold and silver coins in monetary transactions. These money changers set up shop on long tables with benches on either side; the word bank comes from the old French *banc*, meaning bench. Initially, "although the money changers' paper receipts and book entries could be used as a currency, their production had to be (pre-)*financed* by savings deposits."[2] In order to issue credit, in other words, lenders required an equal amount of coins. But once people became accustomed to paper receipts and book entries over gold and silver, the banks were able to issue credits that exceeded their actual reserves, giving rise to the fractional reserve system, wherein banks keep a predetermined percentage of total reserves on hand.

Eventually, even those fractional reserves were outsourced to central banks: "commercial banks' 'reserves' were now merely payment pledges on the part of the central bank, meaning that any trader, company or employee depositing money with a bank no longer received a promise of silver or gold, but a promise of a promise." In 1971, the United States terminated the convertibility of the U.S. dollar to gold bullion, marking the collapse of the Bretton Woods Agreement and the emergent era of floating exchange rates. "Today," Sahr writes, "central bank reserves consist of substance-less book entries just like those in a private bank account." Economists describe this as a 'fiat money system',

2    Aaron Sahr, *Keystroke Capitalism: How Banks Create Money for the Few*, Verso Books, 2022, p. 57.

meaning one in which all currency, including reserves, consists of nothing more than written bank debts." This progression—from equal reserves, to fractional reserves, to central bank reserves, to spreadsheets and pure vibes—"has changed capitalism more fundamentally than is generally acknowledged."

Sahr is not the first to imply that conventional wisdom is unequipped for the "substance-less" circus of global finance. As the late David Graeber wrote in December 2019[3]:

> There is a growing feeling, among those who have the responsibility of managing large economies, that the discipline of economics is no longer fit for purpose... Yet the language of public debate, and the wisdom conveyed in economic textbooks, remain almost entirely unchanged... Mainstream economists nowadays might not be particularly good at predicting financial crashes, facilitating general prosperity, or coming up with models for preventing climate change, but when it comes to establishing themselves in positions of intellectual authority, unaffected by such failings, their success is unparalleled.

Writing in the same magazine one year and one global pandemic later, Pankaj Mishra compared the "intellectual trauma" of Western liberalism to Jonathan Lear's study of the Crow Indians[4]:

> Forced to move in the mid-nineteenth century from a nomadic to a settled existence, they catastrophically lost not only their immemorial world but also "the conceptual resources" to understand their past and present. The problem for a Crow Indian, Lear writes, wasn't just that "my way of life has come to an end." It was that "I no longer have the concepts with which to understand myself or the world.... I have *no idea* what is going on."

3     David Graeber, "Against Economics," *New York Review of Books*, December 2019
4     Pankaj Mishra, "Grand Illusions," *New York Review of Books*, November 2020

In his sweeping *Debt: The First 5,000 Years*, Graeber argues that historically, excessive indebtedness leads to social unrest and revolution. Sahr adds that the much-discussed phenomenon of "financialization" is primarily about debt: "investing debts in more debts is the defining business model of a financial services company." Indeed, the total value of loans and other debt instruments exploded from 12 trillion dollars in 1980 to around 240 trillion in 2015, dwarfing the growth rate of the real economy. [5] The reasonable question to ask, then, is where does all this debt come from?

For traditional economists, the answer is savings; they believe that banks issue loans based on their deposits; just like the money changers in Medieval Europe. Here's German finance minister Wolfgang Schäuble: "one person saves money; another needs money. This has to be organized. It's called banking." And Nobel Prize-winner Eugene Fama, synthesizing the Chicago school's position: "People who get credit have to get it from somewhere. Does a credit bubble mean that people save too much during that period? I don't know what a credit bubble means." [6]

Sahr exposes the absurdity of such statements. If available credit is ballooning relative to economic output, the relationship between savings and loans cannot be one-to-one. Instead, as growth and wages stagnate for all but the wealthiest few, ordinary people take on more and more debt — in the form of mortgages, student loans, credit cards, etc. — to afford the mass-produced, aspirational lifestyle neoliberalism promised to provide them. This credit, obviously, isn't financed by their own savings. Instead,

> [P]rivate banks do not even consider whether they have sufficient deposits to cover loans: they simply create new money on credit… If you pay for a purchase with your overdraft, a debit will appear in your account, but the

5       Kathrin Brandmeir, Michaela Grimm and Arne Holzhausen, *Allianz Global Wealth Report 2015*, Munich, 2015.
6       John Cassidy, "Interview with Eugene Fama," *The New Yorker*, January 2010.

credit transferred to the seller's account has not been taken from anyone else — *it has been created from scratch.* All it takes to approve a consumer loan for the purchase of a car (or the purchase of a share by a bank) is to enter a number on a computer keyboard.

That number is now a financial asset, which can be securitized, bundled, swapped, and leveraged at the bank's discretion. Keystroke capitalism, as defined by Sahr, is this "exceptional situation in which capital can be created ex nihilo."

*

*"David Hume, the greatest skeptic of them all, once remarked that after a gathering of skeptics met to proclaim the veracity of skepticism as a philosophy, all of the members of the gathering nonetheless left by the door rather than the window."*

Philip K. Dick

From mainstream op-eds to black pilled message boards, it's often said that the crux of our present crisis is a *failure of imagination.* Frederic Jameson famously wrote in 1996 that "it seems to be easier for us today to imagine the thoroughgoing deterioration of the earth and of nature than the breakdown of late capitalism."[7] Mark Fisher equally famously paraphrased Jameson's aphorism, writing that "it is easier to imagine the end of the world than the end of capitalism."[8] Fisher's riff can now be found emblazoned on algorithmically recommended t-shirts and decorative lighting fixtures.

Sahr's book is a convincing portrait of a financial system where imagination runs wild, so long as it's in the service of the uber rich getting uber richer. As he puts it, "Not everything that happens in modern economies is capitalist in nature, nor is everything that happens within capitalism economic." In fact, by

---

7      Frederic Jameson, *The Seeds of Time,* Columbia University Press: New York, 1994.

8      Mark Fisher, *Capitalist Realism: Is There No Alternative?*, Zero Books, 2009.

focusing on large banks and financial conglomerates, Sahr stops short of a more radical conclusion. It isn't just banks that can create fortunes from nothing; it's anyone with a little money and an internet connection.

During an April 2022 interview, financial journalist Matt Levine asked investment-banker-turned-cryptocurrency-magnate Sam Bankman-Fried about "yield farming", an opaque cryptocurrency scheme popular at the height of the pandemic's digital asset craze. Here is Bankman-Fried's attempt to explain yield farming, worth quoting at length only because it offers a remarkable view inside the capitalist imagination:

> Let me give you sort of like a really toy model of it… You start with a company that builds a box and in practice this box, they probably dress it up to look like a life-changing, you know, world-altering protocol… Maybe for now actually ignore what it does or pretend it does literally nothing. It's just a box… It doesn't do anything but let you put things in it if you so choose. And then this protocol issues a token, we'll call it whatever, 'X token.'
>
> And then you say, alright, well, you've got this box and you've got X token and the box protocol declares… anyone who goes, takes some money, puts it in the box, each day they're gonna airdrop, you know, 1% of the X token pro rata amongst everyone who's put money in the box. That's for now, what X token does, it gets given away to the box people. And now what happens? … In the world that we're in, if you do this, everyone's gonna be like, 'Ooh, box token. Maybe it's cool. If you buy an inbox token,' you know, that's gonna appear on Twitter and it'll have a $20 million market cap.

At this point, Levine interrupts: "Wait, wait, wait, from first principles, it should be zero." By first principles, he means that money is a real thing, procured by toil or genius or worthiness, that markets are reasonably efficient and neutral, and that, as is still taught in Econ 101 classrooms across the world, a society is comprised of homines economici, rational individuals making formulaic decisions.

Bankman-Fried counters that while such a response is "completely reasonable," empirically, the magic box would have value. His imagination isn't subject to the same theoretical hemming. He continues:

> And now all of a sudden everyone's like, wow, people just decide to put $200 million in the box. This is a pretty cool box, right? Like this is a valuable box as demonstrated by all the money that people have apparently decided should be in the box. And who are we to say that they're wrong about that? Like, you know, this is, I mean boxes can be great. Look, I love boxes as much as the next guy. And so then, you know, X token price goes way up. And now it's a $130 million market cap token because of, you know, the bullishness of people's usage of the box. And now all of a sudden of course, the smart money's like, oh, wow, this thing's now yielding like 60% a year in X tokens. Of course I'll take my 60% yield, right? So they go and pour another $300 million in the box and you get a psych and then it goes to infinity. And then everyone makes money.

Levine is dumbfounded: "I think of myself as like a fairly cynical person. And that was so much more cynical than how I would've described farming. You're just like, well, I'm in the Ponzi business and it's pretty good." Again, Bankman-Fried agrees that this is "reasonable." After all, he asks, is this decoupling of market value and real value any different than the Reddit posters pumping meme stocks like GameStop and AMC? It's a clever gambit by the man who at the time was the world's youngest decabillionare.[9]

---

9      11 months after the interview, and 6 months after my first draft of this piece, Bankman-Fried was indicted in U.S. District Court on charges including wire fraud, commodities fraud, securities fraud, money laundering, and campaign finance law violations; he was released on $250 million bond to the Palo Alto home of his parents, which also serves as the collateral backing

Sure, he may have gotten rich from hyping pixie dust, but everyone's doing it. At least, everyone is smart enough to realize that there's no such thing as first principles. We can all be keyboard capitalists.

*

In March of 2017, I received a late-night email on my dormitory listserv with the subject line: "Like gambling but hate the house edge?"

The body of the missive contained precise, complex instructions for purchasing the cryptocurrency known as Ethereum (ETH). Without context, every step listed seemed transparently fraudulent; acquiring this unknown virtual currency involved handing over bank account and social security information to websites with sketchy domains, downloading third-party apps for a "secure digital wallet," and so on. Following the instructions were several indecipherable price graphs with overlapping, jagged lines to support my upstairs neighbor's investment thesis: though very few people were paying attention, he had strong reason to believe the price of Ethereum was about to skyrocket; there was an almost unquantifiable upside. The email ended with several warnings about the extreme risks of buying cryptocurrency; nobody should risk more than they could afford to lose, though personally, the author of the email implied that he was all in, to use his metaphor.

I read the email in bed, intrigued. I *did* like gambling, and hate the house edge. On the other hand, my only knowledge of cryptocurrency was derived from friends who'd used Bitcoin to purchase fake IDs and off-brand stimulants. Then there was the chance that my neighbor had been hacked, overserved, or worse. I deleted the email.

A week later the price of one ETH token broke $20 for the first time; nine months later in January 2018 the price was $1400, a 7000% increase; in November 2021 ETH surpassed $4600, up 23000% or 230x since the time of the e-mail. In more concrete terms, a $100 investment in March 2017 could have been sold for roughly $7000 in 2018 or $23,000 in late 2021.

the bond.

Even after last summer's much-publicized "correction," the price of Ethereum stands around $1900. One way to read this story is that I was offered a rigged slot machine and detailed instructions for how to pull the lever, and I declined, along with nearly everyone else who received the email.

Near the end of the school year, as Ethereum entered the early stages of its parabolic rise, rumors emerged about my clairvoyant neighbor. The number was inconclusive—hundreds of thousands, or maybe millions—but his bet paid off, big time, and he'd disappeared from the dorm. He was running a high-profile hedge fund, or living in Costa Rica, or writing cryptic investment blogs on Medium. The truth was more banal. He'd been found in the dorm's computer cluster overdosing on LSD. When the paramedics arrived he was throwing up, but stable, and as they took him away, the screen was still open to his account balance, a green graph pointing towards infinity.

\*

*"It is the absence of the threat of individual starvation which makes primitive society, in a sense, more human than market economy, and at the same time less economic."*

Karl Polyani, The Great Transformation

To defend the massive wealth disparities produced by liberal market economies, theorists from John Locke to Freidrich Hayek to Milton Friedman have argued that any income is just so long as it is obtained under just conditions. This convenient formulation still depends on a more fundamental question: what are just conditions? One way to think about it is how much someone has to lose. Everyone roots for the gambler, but only the true capitalist roots for the casino.

In his concluding chapter, Sahr warns against framing an analysis of keystroke capitalism with easy dichotomies like economic liberalism and conservatism, or the free market and democracy. "The real question is who is entitled to the privilege of creating money from nothing, or who can be reasonably entrusted with it." "In the world's advanced economies," Sahr writes, "companies are increasingly generating their income from investments in financial assets, to the detriment of their actual core business, and hence also to the detriment of investments in real capital such as raw materials, machinery or labour." The separation between real goods and services and their financial representations is not merely a side-effect; as DeBord writes, "*separation* is the alpha and omega of the spectacle." In the age of keystroke capitalism, tech companies are financial companies, car companies are financial companies, universities are financial companies, web3 projects are financial companies, hospitals are financial companies, and so on.

"Almost immediately," Borges writes in *Tlön, Uqbar, Orbis Tertius*, "reality gave ground on more than one point. The truth is that it hankered to give ground." Now that the secret is out, there's no turning back; the creation of debt instruments continues to overshadow output, and anyone looking to get properly rich must join in the exploitation and pursuit of alchemy. Like a balloon snipped from a dumbbell, the value of nothing will rise ever higher above the value of something.

# Looking at Sparrows Through a Trellis
Colin Myrea

The hydrangeas are dead.
The petals, brown crisping at the blue edges
Prised by the wind and deposited
At the foot of one ignoring it.

Gathered, some in shade
And others around the clouded
Plastic feeder, in a
Column of writhing feathers.

The unblinking wooden eye.

# Jocasta's Noose
Colin Myrea

The black veil came over my eyes:
I was standing alone
& mirthful in that long, white room
With the empty wicker
That was empty but for the lamb
An empty smirk on its lips.

# Weary & Delighted
Colin Myrea

He rode through town, on a great black horse
Champing at smoke, oak leaves in his hair.

I saw him kill them, the great hands that tore
And the foot that cut on the headless crown

But did not throw myself before him,

61

Though I wish I had been under heel as well.

# Geese on Film
Colin Myrea

I don't mind, you know.
Waiting between red petals
During soft May rain
The pictures don't do justice
The plaster is so lifelike.

# Patrick Modiano: Haunted by Memories
GD Dess

*"Memory is already a story, and when there are gaps in memory, new stories must be confabulated to fill in the holes."*

Mark Fisher

French author Patrick Modiano turned seventy-eight this July. His literary output, beginning in his early twenties, has been prodigious: he has written more than 30 works of fiction, as well as screenplays for films (*Lacombe, Lucien* co-written with Louis Malle), children's books, and memoirs. He was awarded the Nobel Prize in literature in 2014 "for the art of memory with which he has evoked the most ungraspable human destinies..." Often referred to as existential detective stories, Modiano's novels are both atmospheric and enigmatic, combining, as poet and literary critic Adam Kirsch has noted, "a detective's curiosity with an elegist's melancholy."

Despite his Nobel, and despite the availability of his translated work, Modiano is not well known in the United States. One wonders why. Is there a particularly European aspect to his melancholy? Do Americans yawn in the face of memory? In his Nobel speech, Modiano noted that memory "is in a constant struggle against amnesia and oblivion," and posited that "we can only pick up fragments of the past, disconnected traces, fleeting and almost ungraspable human destinies." It would therefore seem that this is not a European phenomenon, but a human one, which is why Modiano puts at the center of his work. Reading his novels sensitizes us to a reality we may have only dimly perceived, which is that while we typically think of memories as immutable objects we preserve throughout our lives, and often cherish, this is not the case. Memories are not immortal: like people and things, they are subject to vanishing, like life itself they fade and die and, in the end, abandon us.

Memory occupies an odd place in our consciousness, somewhere between reality and dream. What our memories hold, how we maintain them, or find them when they seem to have disappeared—and how we verify that they are correct if we find them—are the subjects about which Modiano writes. His protagonists unearth names and dates, they search through old telephone directories and police files, they try to verify addresses, locate pictures, in an effort to construct real or imaginary narratives, generally of people who have gone missing.

For Modiano the tragedy of human life is that memories are mortal: they degrade over time and disappear, abandoning us just like people. Modiano knows that loss, abandonment, and the threat of vanishing is the fate we all suffer. For, like his characters, every day we, too, are abandoned: loved ones pass away, children leave home, our significant other leaves us, or we leave them, our memory fails us, our friends unfriend us. His stories, which engage memory on every level, are told without sentimentality or emotion (the lack of which some readers find unnerving) and portray the struggle in which we are all engaged as we work to keep our lives in balance in the face of ongoing losses.

These ideas are in full bloom in Modiano's most recent works, *The Black Notebook* (2016), *Invisible Ink* (2020), and *Scene of the Crime* (2023) all admirably translated by Mark Polizzotti. The narrators in these novels are named Jean (which is Modiano's first name) and rely on jottings in notebooks (a typical Modiano ploy) to aid in their search for a missing person. In *The Black Notebook,* Jean revisits his 50-year-old black notebook in which he had recorded certain events: "a succession of names, phone numbers, appointments, and also short texts that might have something to do with literature," which portray the aimless, peripatetic life he led in Paris during his early 20's, and his involvement with a mysterious woman named Dannie, who disappeared. In *Invisible Ink,* Jean steals a black notebook from the room of Noëlle Lefebvre whom he is seeking to locate after her disappearance from Paris thirty years earlier. This notebook, too, contains fragments of information, nothing more than seemingly unrelated pieces of a puzzle that the narrator struggles to put together in his search for the missing woman.

Modiano's novels typically involve the narrator's search for someone he knew in his youth who had a profound effect upon his life. More often than not, the missing individuals are women. They tend to be distant, fragile, and prone to suicide. Modiano's male characters are often shady drifters or grifters, or detectives or former detectives, as in *Invisible Ink*. Both the women and men exist on the periphery of respectable bourgeois society. In *The Black Notebook*, Jean describes himself as existing outside respectability: "I had no credit, no legitimacy. No family or defined social status. I floated on the Paris air." In *Invisible Ink*, Jean appears to be unemployed, possibly a writer, but at one point he says, ironically, he is a history professor.

*The Black Notebook* revolves around Jean's attempt to discover what became of Dannie. He describes her as "no more than a spot of light, without relief, as in an overexposed photograph. A blank." She has no family to speak of, no permanent address, no visible means of support. She associates with a group of "losers"—members of the "Montparnasse gang." Various members of the gang aid and abet her existence; they procure her a room in the hotel where they meet, allow her the use of a car, and one of them provides her with false identity papers. What she does for them in return is left unsaid.

As in almost all of Modiano's novels, the setting of *The Black Notebook* is Paris, the city in which Modiano was born, and the city that continues to fascinate him. Modiano has said that "Themes of disappearance, identity and the passing of time are closely bound up with the topography of cities." In a city, anyone can disappear if they want to. Anyone can change their identity by adopting an alias.[10] Jean and Dannie spend most of their time together, desultorily wandering the streets of Paris. They live in

10    Dannie goes by several aliases, including Mireille Sampierry, Michèle Aghamouri, and Jeannine de Chillaud. Her real name is Dominique Roger.

shabby rooms in cheap hotels. They have no place to call home. They exist in the present, seeking to avoid the "menace that hovered over everything." This menace emanates from the sketchy people with whom they associate, and from the more abstract, but, in its own way, equally perilous bourgeois society, with its stultifying rules and codes of behavior. In some sense, the couple is always on the lam.

Toward the end of *The Black Notebook* one of the "Montparnasse gang" warns Jean that Dannie was mixed up in something pretty serious, a "nasty incident," and that she might be held accountable. He won't reveal what it is. When Jean asks Dannie about it, she says, "Do I really look like someone who'd get involved in a nasty incident?" Reflecting on her response 50 years later, Jean says: "I believe that already, back then, I had understood that no one ever answers questions."

The story line in *Invisible Ink* revolves around a notebook that the narrator, Jean Eyben, steals from the room of a woman for whom he has been searching. The woman's name is Noëlle Lefebvre. She came to Paris 30 years ago, stayed several months, then vanished. Jean was first introduced to her through a "fact sheet," a scant three paragraphs of data points that his boss gave him to begin the search. Working as a detective ("on a trial basis") at the Huette Detective Agency at the time, it was his job to find her and establish her true identity, a task at which he failed. Upon leaving the agency, he took her case file with him, as a souvenir, and it is to this file that he returns all these years later to attempt to fill in the "blanks" in her case. The details, scant though they are, are sufficient to put the narrative in motion.

Who is Noëlle Lefebvre? What happened to her? How does this "person of interest" connect to Jean's life? The story that unfurls seeks to answer these questions, which become increasingly pressing as Jean comes to feel that Noëlle may form a "missing link" in his own life.

From Huette's case file and from the stolen notebook, Jean begins to piece together the stray fragments to form a picture of her Parisian existence. We learn about her boyfriend Sancho (real name, Serge) and his Chrysler convertible; a failed actor who went by the name of Gérard Mourade; their flashy friend Brainos and La Marine Dance Club; a poem: "The sky is, above the roof/So calm, so fair!/A branch, above the roof/Fans the air"(which may be, my own research has determined, a corrupted partial version of Paul Verlaine's poem *The Sky Above the Roof*); and, that she grew up in a small provincial town, Annecy—a town in which the narrator also spent time.

To solve this case and the mystery of Noëlle's life Jean must fit together all the pieces of the puzzle he's accumulated so "that the whole picture might emerge, more or less." The narration moves backwards and forwards in time as memory and reality reveal new data points about her life. While he feels as if he is making progress, he worries that the details he's gathered about Noëlle "remind me of the crackling of static in a telephone, growing louder and louder. It keeps you from hearing a voice calling to you from far away."

Modiano has said that he has always been writing the same novel (on fait toujours le même roman) and his most recent work, *Scene of the Crime* (2023) doesn't disappoint on that score. As in the previous two novels, this one, too, centers around a notebook, a blue one. While not his most successful work, partially because late in the story (while hinted at earlier), for no necessary reason, we encounter a metafictional twist in which the narrator, Jean Bosmans, who is rather weakly drawn, turns out to be an author himself—of the story we're reading.

Drawing from his memory, Bosmans writes a multitude of details in his notebook seeking to find the common thread among them that will help him remember an event he witnessed that happened fifty years in the past. Finding the key that will unlock that memory may involve an overheard phrase, "Guy has just gotten out of prison." Like other Modiano narrators Bosmans knows "he'd been used to living in the narrow margin between reality and dream, letting them illuminate each other, sometimes blend together." Pursued by three shady characters who want to know what he knows about what happened in a house on Rue du Docteur-Kurzenne, time itself is a bigger worry for Jean because, "Little by little, time had erased the different periods of his life, none of which had a connection with the subsequent one, and as such that life had been only a series of interruptions, avalanches, or even amnesias."

Because Modiano's protagonists recognize that our memories are fragile and ephemeral, they live in a state of existential emergency in which they attempt to fill the "blanks" and "missing links" before the corrosive effects of time completely dissolve them. Like Modiano's characters we, too, recognize, if only tacitly, that our lives are a series of ongoing "interruptions, avalanches, or even amnesias." It is this recognition that produces the unique melancholy frisson of pleasure of reading Modiano.[11]

---

11    While this essay has centered around Modiano's most recent work, for readers interested in experiencing the pleasure of 'Modiano melancholy' I might also suggest some of his earlier novels, such as: *Missing Person* (1978), for which he won the Prix Goncourt, in which a detective suffering from amnesia seeks his own identity; the novel opens with the portentous sentence "I am Nothing"; and, *Out of the Dark* (1995) in which the narrator takes off from Paris for London after committing a crime at the behest of a mysterious woman named Jacqueline, who is not beyond exchanging sex for money, and who then abandons him in London for another man. Their paths cross years later in Paris and he discovers her real name may be Thérèse Caisley, but after a brief tryst she disappears again without him learning any more about her than the day he met her.

# Yahoo Boys, New Style
Noah Kumin

These were the ideas that obsessed me at the time: that love
is a sham, that honor's a cheat, that art is no more than public
self-diddling for the benefit of a voyeuristic bourgeoisie; that
happiness is mere stupidity and beauty a beast (every lovely body
a time capsule of dust and worms); that the soul's only a poetic
fiction meant to distract from the slowly curdling blood and bile
that are truly at the center of us all. We've all been exposed to
these ideas at one point or another. The difference is that most
people have the good sense to blink and move on. Philosophers,
on the other hand—by which I mean, in my own case, adjunct
Lecturers in Communications with a penchant for political theory—manage to screw up their eyes at the words till their faces get
stuck like that. No wonder I found myself in adulthood unable to
emit real tears. Probably all those little Loeb editions did damage
to my ducts. I often longed afterwards for the old catharsis of it,
but, in lieu of any onions handy, would have to settle for getting
drunk on a pint of Seagrams and falling over somewhere unex-
pected.

    If this has already begun to sound a bit like a mad ad-
junct's monograph or, worse, an arty *mea culpa*, it's only that I
want to underline here one important fact: All I ever meant to do
was read books about the world and meekly, caustically despise
it. I never meant to actually enlarge its evil. More specifically, I
never meant to find myself on a plane to Helsinki at the tail-end
of a snowstorm, primping my fake mustache as I prepared to
rendezvous with the soft-skinned midwestern widow who had
fallen in love with me—and from whom, I should add, I'd stolen
upwards of $30,000. But the Lord works in mysterious ways. The
devil does too, of course. But the mystery about him is, as with
any charming sociopath, is not the pattern of his behavior. It's
how we ever fell for him in the first place.

    Probably my life's first evil omen was an inborn hatred of
the climate in which I was raised. Gainesville, Florida, is muggy
even in November; by June you can feel your very pores congeal.

My first childish conception of heaven, crayoned with loving care onto construction paper at my ill-attended eighth birthday party, was of a utopian North Pole, where parents and children and out-of-place geckoes all lived together as frigid equals. My real-life father was one of those tinker-happy, ineffectual men predisposed to alcoholism and whole days spent on old canoes MacGyvered for the ideal transport of Natty Ice twelve-packs. Obviously mom tired of this pretty quickly. She left him when I was seven and took up with a real estate developer. Soon enough they became (and here's the true key to happiness for American marriages) business partners as well as lovers, and built a huge glassy house on the shores of Tuscawilla Lake.

Another factor may well be my face. It's sometimes said in jest that redheads constitute an alien species; my own appearance has done little to dispel this unfortunate prejudice. For all I know I came straight out of the womb with that scaly eczema on the bridge of my nose and fiery neck-beard. My complexion is something like the color of raw whale flesh. My body type is and has been, long before the paradoxical neologism entered popular consciousness, skinny-fat.

So I spent a lot of time indoors as a child. Some dropouts from the University of Florida (a college-themed amusement park at the center of town) had conspired to make Gainesville a radical hub in the '70s. The last trace of their efforts was the Civic Media Center, a musty-smelling, halfway-alphabetized community library just a stone's throw from Gator Beverage. Beginning one rainy afternoon in October '98, when Bogdan, the post-punk who presided over the place, greeted my entrance with a demure hem-lift of his blue velvet dress, the building became a second home to me. I devoured my way from Abu-Jamal to Žižek over the next few years, with a special emphasis on the Narodnik circle of Russian revolutionaries.

In '02, I went off to a fancy college in the Northeast. In '04 dad had a stroke. That winter I returned home to nurse him and transferred to UF, peddling my Schwinn nightly between the library and inpatient wing of the university hospital, where applesauce dribbled eternally down his quavering lower lip. He died only a few months after the properties over which my stepdad had been slumlording defaulted, in February of 2008.

Next came New York, grad school, adjuncting, penury. As of this past Spring, I'd been splitting a roach-friendly basement studio with an anarchist who made his share of the rent by orchestrating "non-events." These consisted mostly in the twirling of marionettes made from the bones of baby rats and the blowing of kazoos through both nostrils at once. When he informed me one cloudless Sunday morning, with as much tact as he could muster, that a downtown gallery had expressed interest in his found art and that he'd be moving out at the end of the month to an above-ground residence, I figured the time had come to make a change. Without so much as a text goodbye to him or anyone, I blew $523 of my $987.43 savings on a one-way ticket to St. Petersburg, Russia, where I knew the stories of many dead radicals, but no living souls.

The cabbie at the airport started things off right by spotting my pocket Russian-English dictionary and fleecing me for twelve times the standard fare. In the city center, I drank my first vodka-soda-in-a-can. Already I felt both elated and queasy. And though I'd read plenty about the White Nights in books, I was still caught off guard when the evening sun did not set, but instead diffused itself somehow into the city's very architecture, turning every column, capstone and cornice the color of fever dream. After two days in a hostel in the old part of town—all car exhaust and iridescent canals—I found cheaper lodgings in the exurbs, on the wide-berthed Korablstroitelei (Of or Relating to Shipbuilders) Boulevard. The room looked out onto the turgid sea. I felt at peace. But my rubles were dwindling, so I began to trawl Russian Craigslist, where I soon came across a job listing that appeared at the time to be no less a miracle than the Star of the Sea.

The firm's name was "Global Fulfillment Corp." Its ad stated in both Russian and an unorthodox version of my own native tongue that the company "will wish to summon proficient-English speakers for cyber and various communications." Beyond that, the details were as muddy as the syntax, but the words "large money" and "with good hope for growth" were printed clearly enough at the bottom, and so I filled out the e-form with care.

In the field under "Political Preferences" I wrote 'anarcho-communism, in the tradition of Kropotkin,' and then, after thinking for a moment, appended: "but willing to work constructively with statists." Under "Past Communications Experience" I checked both "Polemical" and "Pedagogical." And in response to the directive "Please list any significant social ties or organizations to which applicant currently belongs," I typed, simply, "N/A." Within a few hours I received a message requesting an interview.

The building made up the eastern wing of a sickly yellow neoclassical affair called Bobrinsky (Of or Relating to Beavers) Palace. It was and still is, as far as I know, under strenuous renovation. In the front hallway I was immediately greeted by a doe-eyed construction worker who took my entry as an opportunity to begin drilling a plinth, and a bulldog-faced guard who demanded to see some form of ID I had never heard of. Our witty repartee went on for a good twenty minutes. It consisted mostly of my muttering to myself while the guard shouted "*identifikatsiya*," almost contrapuntally with the drill's bracing solo. I was suddenly reminded of the basketball court outside my exurban window, where each night five blonde boys in capris (I imagined they were always the same boys, though I could never confirm it) would pass the ball interminably around the perimeter without even looking at the hoop.

It was only after a slight, anemic-looking man about my age had shuffled outside to the courtyard to smoke that I got the idea to see if he might intervene—at which point he introduced himself in English as Vova, CEO and sole employee of the Global Corp.

"Normally you can smoke inside," he said, "but the electricians are here repairing a fuse and ask I must go out of doors. They are idiots but I humor them."

"I don't smoke," I said.

"You will. Do you like Kvass?"

"Never tried it."

"Vodka?"

"Very much so."

"Fine. You are a fast typer?"

"Over 150 words per minute."

"And you have a deep voice. That's good. Like a toad almost. There is a 24-hour store on the corner for vital needs and a pancake stand at the bus stop. For piss and shit use the bathroom past the front hallway. Anything more private and you may use a separate toilet, on the basement level. Do you have questions?"

"Um, is there any paperwork?"

Vova laughed—a quiet, listless little laugh.

My first shift lasted sixteen hours. Vova introduced me to three cranky American citizens—all of them fictitious—whose minds I would be inhabiting and whose bile I would diligently spew. Still-spry septuagenarian Timothy Bryant, for instance, tended bar in Albuquerque, while Melissa Reviati, 33, of Binghamton, NY, had herself a solid little practice up there as an internist. (The mysterious 42-year-old Victor Grachis was self-employed in Kalamazoo). What the three of them had in common was a distinct anti-American bent, with a corresponding leniency toward Mother Russia's foibles. Along with all this came a certain tendency toward catastrophism and divisiveness when any sort of difficult political issue hit the New World's shores. While I was there, all three were positively panicked over Ebola.

It was, in brief, a troll farm—nestled on the banks of the bubbling Moika (Little Quagmire) River, in the pleasant vale of swampland that Peter the Great had choked into civilization centuries ago for just this purpose. I took turns between Facebook, Instagram, and Twitter, tossing as many strings of text as I could @ prominent journalists and local authorities. Timing and volume were key, hence the long shifts. Vova, who did not seem to have left the premises for at least a decade, showed me where to find the instant coffee. Evening sun filtered in like sludge through the dust-covered window panes. Part of the job was to maintain the reality of my cyphers, so, by the eleventh hour, I was posting mostly about each one's cat. Both bathrooms came in handy.

At my 6 A.M. clock-out I went over to Vova's desk where he remained implacably fixed to the screen.

"Do I come in tomorrow?" I asked.

"Why wouldn't you?"

"What time?"

"Evening news cycle in the U.S. begins at five, so noon is our time."

"You've got to be kidding me."

"No I do not. Were I kidding you I would slap you on the back and say, for instance, haha."

"You would?"

"It is possible. It has been a long time since I've been kidding. I recommend the couch in the basement level. The long bench by the bus stop is also comfortable, when the weather is moderate. Now before I forget, write for me your bank account and routing numbers. You will find a deposit there when time comes."

I didn't have the strength to resist. Sixty-six hours later, after three more sixteen-hour shifts spaced out by six-hour breaks, during which time Vova had come up with the idea to use my uninflected English-speaking voice for various 'podcasts,' I took the bus back to my exurb, walked alone through the lamplight of my long, oval-shaped boulevard, briefly considered bashing my skull in against the pedestal of Cultural Commissar Lunacharsky's handsome likeness, and then turned in for the night. And day. And night again. I slept till 9 P.M. the following evening. Apparently a thunderstorm had just ended. Pink and gold rainclouds, too vivid for comfort, skipped from puddle to puddle across the badly leveled court below. Already those nocturnal little pricks in capris were back at it, tossing the ball idiotically back and forth.

"Shoot," I muttered to myself, "for God's sake, one of you please shoot"—and brought up my banking app, where I discovered that a deposit had been made for 350,000 rubles—what was then just over $10,000.

A new era had begun. I had not had as much as ten grand to my name for the last decade. I thought back to those graduate seminars at the New School, for which I'd been paid a cool $3,000 per semester to highlight distinctions between anarcho-syndicalism and anarcho-primitivism in Gramsci or Murray Bookchin. Now the sum had been more than tripled for four days straight of "America=illuminati devilbitch."

I celebrated my newfound success by downing a half-liter of Baltiïskaya Volna (Tide of the Baltic) vodka and going back to sleep. When I woke up again it was time for work.

"There is a problem," Vova said at the entranceway, "we are decommissioned for a time. I'm afraid I worked too hard. Authorities have flagged your cyphers. Last night I received memoranda from the cultural apparatus relaying that your work is to be put on hold."

I gaped at him, crestfallen.

"But do not become sad," Vova said, "I have been preparing a side-project for just someone of your type. It is not guaranteed to work but I have big hopes. Have you heard of, for example, Yahoo Boys?"

I shook my head no.

"They were not trolls exactly but scam artists. Mostly 419 scams and the like. You know, they write to say they are Nigerian princes in need of quick cash which they will later redouble."

"But they don't actually redouble?"

"Do not be an idiot. It is quite opposite. Once the victims have paid a small amount they will pay more and more and more—just to convince themselves they have made a correct decision in the first place. It is human psychology. The scammers were called Yahoo Boys because of early success using such email domains. But they left many possible stones unturned. You and I will become the foundation of Yahoo Boys, new style."

"Meaning?"

"Tell me," Vova said, curling his lips into a snarl, "are you much of a romantic?"

During my philosophical years I had taken a special inter-

75

est in the techniques and apparatuses by which the notion of love had spread itself throughout the western world. From good old fascist Plato, who knew at his heart's core that love could exist only between a man of culture and the young boy he was penetrating, to that true romantic Andreas Capellanus, who ushered in the age of chivalry with his comment that true love for one's spouse is impossible because it is an act of duty, to the recent politicization of love, whereby the world's oligarchs could splatter the phrase "Love Wins" across bank branches and army barracks alike.

I told Vova that he was talking to the right guy.

He led me over to his laptop and showed me photos of a kindly-looking, middle-aged woman with chunky blonde streaks in her hair and crocuses in her lawn.

"This is Buffi," Vova said, "she lives in the American town of Terre Haute. Tell her something romantic."

I paused for a moment, staring at Buffi's match.com answers ("I enjoy going out and being social, eating at restaurants and getting a drink at a fun bar. I like to travel and see new places") and idyllic thumbnail photo of her musing among the vegetables.

"You want me to help you rob this woman?"

"Seduce and rob. Seduce comes first. This is important."

"I would feel bad."

"Do not feel bad. Think of you and her as just pixels. Pixels do not have feelings."

I typed: "Tonight even the shadows of the poplar trees seem to be swaying in unison with that ineffable, otherworldly force that presides over the ways of the heart."

"This is not philosophy school, you American faggot. Write something stronger. Shorter and stronger."

"You exude a beautiful spirit," I tried.

Vova sighed.

"Perhaps you will sleep on it."

But that wasn't even necessary. Buffi and I—by which I mean Buffi and Chester van Rockland, originally of Buxton, Derbyshire, UK, but lately transferred for work reasons to Terre

Haute—were made for each other, and she messaged us first:

"We are listed as a Perfect Match! I'm not sure exactly what this means. Would you be interested in me, first of all? Check my profile, I guess."

Vova had outfitted my cypher with a salt-and-pepper beard, Wayfarers and enigmatic profession: Systems Analyst. How could we fail?

"We will wait exactly two days before we write," he said, "then is necessary to solicit email address and delete the profile page. I will take the lead in writing, you simply edit for grammar and culture."

It worked like a charm—or a curse. With our powers combined, we came up with such gems as:

"You fill the space between my fingers. I can't wait to hold your hand and walk along the sandy beaches of the lake at sunset. Just remind yourself that you fill those spaces. Whenever you feel sad or mad—just remember! You are my princess."

The em-dash was my favorite part.

Vova planned out the long game. He had me relate early on that I'd have to make an emergency trip to Belgium for work, and lately broke the news that I was a bit of a black sheep here on the continent. You see, it was a tricky time, what with the Greek crisis and that whole rigamarole, so it now seemed (how embarrassing) that my Cyprus-stashed assets were frozen—just until I could hash things out with Dijsselbloem and the rest of those buzzkills in the Eurogroup.

This was a crucial moment. Would she express sympathy? Interest? Or would she get suspicious? Vova worried that the bit about Greece was too au courant, that she might have some personal interest in the matter and ask further questions. I reminded him that this person was an American. Our whole enterprise now hung in the balance. I would soon find out whether Vova was indeed the criminal mastermind he made himself out to be, or just a taciturn insane person who had convinced me to spend months in a poorly ventilated basement, exchanging clichés with an Indiana housewife. As I sat staring at the screen, trying to put it into action, Vova lay a damp hand on my shoulder.

"Do you know what day it is today?" he asked.

"Somewhere between Tuesday and Sunday," I said, "mid-to-late June."

"It is the Day of the Scarlet Sails."

"Which means?"

"Young people will be drunk on the street all night."

"In a way different from usual?"

"Different in one way of great import. On the River Neva will float a schooner conveyed by three scarlet sails. The sails signify success. On this night I must introduce you to a spiritual matter. We'll hurry now. Time is limited."

For a sickly, almost gangrenous small person, Vova walked surprisingly fast. We bustled along the Moika and on toward the city center. The brisk wind and dozen mugs of instant coffee had my heart twinging. Waves from the river lapped in rhythm against their boundary walls, now and then sputtering up toward our feet. The sulfur smell of homemade fireworks mingled with that of street sewage to make for a kind of rotten egg salad.

"Let us sit," Vova said as we approached a bench across a small footbridge. Perched on either side of the bridge were two identical gold-winged griffins, glaring at us with the heavy-lidded impassivity so typical of the inanimate. I asked Vova what kind of spiritual matter he had in mind.

"It is a matter of paramount importance and will decide our fate. But it must wait until midnight. Now it is 11:48."

"Twelve minutes," I sighed.

"I always knew you were intelligent. What was it you said you had been a professor of?"

"Philosophy and Political Theory."

"And what were your learnings?"

"That all of our world institutions are corrupt."

"Idiots and small children know this."

"Well, not just that. There was an experimental aspect. A search for the keys to achieving radical social change."

"Did you find many?"

"Not exactly. The keys are more like, you know, a state of mind. A new style of imagination, a conceptual fearlessness, a readiness to speed without compunction down the blind alleys of thought—without yielding to social pressures and received wisdom of ages past."

"Which is why you are in Russia now, thieving from lonely widows over a wireless connection. Is correct?"

A pretty young woman clomped over in our direction, flashed Vova a smile, and vomited promptly onto the curb. Then she checked her face on her phone and walked off.

"We will approach the bridge now," Vova said.

The griffins, on closer inspection, looked sullen and vindictive. Their beaks appeared to have been carved into sharper edges than were strictly necessary for mere purposes of mimesis.

"We experience now the most auspicious hour of the summer's most auspicious night," he continued. "It is tradition that with the stroke of midnight, you may place a hand in the griffin's mouth and state any sum of money. The griffins will grant you that sum. By my calculations we may reasonably remove $112,000 from the savings of Buffi. You will now insert your hand into the griffin and place our request."

The statue's gullet was cavernous and dry. I wondered what Vova meant by 'reasonably.'

"Well, griffin," I said, "I know we just met, and this is probably as weird for you as it is for me. But sometimes life throws us some crazy surprises, and—"

"You will get to the point," Vova said.

"Griffin, please give me $112,000."

"Remove your hand. All that remains now is to pay the tribute. Simply place a ruble at its feet."

"I don't have any coins on me. Do I have to pay it this second?"

"Is essential to take place at the stroke of midnight. I will run to the store."

"Hurry!" I said.

It was again off-putting to see just how quickly he was capable of moving, while maintaining a comportment of picture-perfect listlessness. Vova's torso seemed somehow always at least one step ahead of his shuffling feet.

"Griffin," I said, "between you and me, I'm beginning to feel a bit sick to my stomach about all this. You seem like you know what's going on here. Please show me the way. . . ."

The griffin didn't even blink. By the time Vova returned with the coins it was 12:02, but our extenuating circumstances must have been acknowledged, because the next day Buffi wrote to ask if there was any way she might help me out of my jam. The worst part was that I was beginning to like her—whatever that could mean under the circumstances. It has been claimed that we can only fall in love with what we don't know about a person, and for all Buffi's discharge of raw information, she remained as mysterious to me as I must have seemed to her. Her earnest affection put me out more than any hot-and-cold coquetry could have. All this was tinged by a sort of wry, muted humor that I could only assume was midwestern ("I guess this is a weird way to meet people," she'd written in one of our first chats, "but at least it's warmer than the dairy aisle at Kohler's"). From there she sometimes veered into the outright Warholian; apropos her crocuses, she told me the chilling story of her friend Maura: "One time she got so into weeding that she spent ten hours a day in the garden for a whole week. She said she didn't want to see even a speck of green that wasn't intentional. Come to think of it, I actually haven't heard from Maura since then. Hopefully she's still alive."

I often thought of Buffi's small, soft-looking hands. She began to appear regularly in my dreams. By the Winter Solstice I'd stolen about $15,000 from her.

Then came a horrible message:

"Have I got a surprise for YOU," Buffi wrote, "I'm treating myself to a vacation! Since those awful men won't let you leave Europe, I figured I'd make things easier and come to you! I fly into Madrid, but just tell me where to meet. We can do anything at all. I know you must have some romantic hotspots up your sleeve."

"This is great news," Vova said, "you will meet her and drive the hook more deep."

"I'll what?" I said.

"We will get you special clothes and makeup. I happen to have several contacts in the theater. How long will it take you to grow a beard?"

"About three weeks."

"You will have to do it faster."

"This isn't going to work, Vova."

"You will put powder in your hairs and beard, and be outfitted with the kind of thick sweater popular among grandpas."

"Just so you know, the last time I tried acting was in a high school drama club when I puked all over the stage."

"And I will find for you spectacles."

If I had felt capable of crying, this would have been a good time. Instead, I just stared into the computer screen until my mind went blank.

I told Buffi we would meet in Helsinki on a Tuesday and then go from there to a Ski & Spa trip up near Lapland. But (wasn't it just my luck?) I ended up getting held at the border. They kept me on lockdown till 6PM the following Monday, leaving only twenty-four hours before I was due back in Brussels for further interrogation. Buffi suggested that we just meet at the Holiday Inn outside the airport. I consented. I figured I could make it work for a night.

All through the flight I ran through fantasies of my failure—these mostly involved roly- poly Finnish policemen shaking the powder from my hair and asking me wasn't I ashamed—but in truth I had begun to feel as much like Chester van Rockford as myself, and by the time I entered fateful room 526 to greet Buffi with a continental *bis bis*, I knew in an instant that this absurd plan could actually work. For a moment the two of us remained standing face-to-face, appraising one another, directly in the middle of the orderly, anesthetized motel room.

Buffi's thick, streaked hair fell straight onto her shoulders, and the ceiling light above her made the faint gray strands at the top of her scalp seem silvery and austere. After a moment she sat, keeping perfect posture, on the edge of the bed, which was covered by a loose-knit cloth comforter patterned in gray paisley. She looked up and trained her large, green eyes on me.

81

"Would you like to sit?"

I sat, leaving a safe eight inches or so between us.

"To see you after so long," she said, "it's almost unbelievable."

I glanced over her shoulder out the window. The neon green lights of the Holiday Inn sign seeped eerily into the pavement and blue-tinged snow. It felt like I was approaching the weird denouement of a nightmare. We made small talk: Europe was beautiful, the flight had been fine. She was simultaneously more demure, more sure of herself than I might have imagined. Her compact body pressed just teasingly enough against the thin fabric of her sweater. I was, pathetically, ridiculously, attracted to her. She leant over to kiss me. I jerked my head away.

"What's wrong?" she said.

My mind seemed to have lost the connection. It was all too much for words. So I did what anyone would have done: I fell back on what came naturally to me.

"Have you ever wondered," I said, "whether maybe we lay too much emphasis on love?"

Buffi furrowed her brow.

"You mean—you and me?" she said.

"No, I mean in general. Whether it, uh, maybe plays an outsize role in the construction of our daily reality. Like as a technique for determining normative social behavior and, um, as a handy container for all non-materialist longings."

The light at the window began to flicker. A draft seeped in from under the pane and tingled the nape of my neck.

"Like: whether the concept of love might function as some kind of sinister vacuum, sucking up all our ideals—by which we might, I don't know, transform society or something— into some useless black hole of procreation and joint income taxes."

A few minutes of silence followed. Finally Buffi said:

"You're not at all like how I imagined you'd be."

The look on her face frightened me. I tried to backtrack.

"Er—it was just something that crossed my mind," I said, "just a new way of thinking about the whole business, like a new

style of art or architecture or whatever. I was just, you know, trying it out. What do you think?"

"I think it's narrow-minded and stupid," Buffi said, "and
was probably invented by someone who's never loved."

Then she got up, walked briskly to the bathroom and
locked the door.

We slept in our clothes that night, on top of the paisley
comforter, spaced as far apart as possible. I rose silently at dawn
and left Buffi a note saying I'd explain it all over email.

When I got home to Korablstroitelei, there was only one
little punk left on the court by the sea, his shadow magnified
monstrously under the lamplight. He was tossing the ball back
and forth against the cement wall by the baseline, from which
point it would return to him on a hop. I got the sense that he had
been doing this continuously for all the time I'd been in Helsinki—maybe taking occasional breaks to scour for shellfish along
the shore. I lay down in my bed and watched him repeat this
hopeless task, as surefire and maddening as a metronome. And
then a miracle occurred. The boy took hold of his ball, dribbled
conscientiously to the top of the key, and squared up toward the
basket. He set his feet apart as wide as his shoulders, cocked his
right elbow, and launched a jumper with absolutely perfect form.
It was an airball.

There is no equivalent in Russian for 'panic attack,' although
nervous exhaustion has plenty of precedent. Back before wifi
rendered the world flat, mountain air had been the cure of choice,
but today the motherland's mentally ill are as thoroughly drugged
as the rest of us. And along with most other useful items in the
country, opioids are best gotten by bribe, so it didn't take long to
find the right palm to grease in exchange for a steady supply of
oxycodone. This, at least, kept the tremors at bay over the next
few months and helped me spend at least twelve hours out of
every twenty-four blissfully unconscious.

One of the strange things about pharma-induced numb-
ness (and it has this in common, I think, with what certain
moralists still refer to as the state of sin), is that part of oneself

remains somehow aloof from the day-to-day turpitude, watching over it all with impatient disgust. So in between long appraisals of my bedspread (off-white and artfully patterned with sweat and drool stains) I managed to write an email to Buffi that told her the truth.

She followed the stages to a tee. First came denial, and the near-daily urgings for me to cut it out with the practical jokes. It was only after I returned the money to her PayPal account that she saw the situation for what it was and moved on to malice. (I sometimes wonder whether she might have despised me less if I hadn't returned the money.) Just about all the unkind things she said about me were based on documentary evidence and true; I see no reason to reproduce them here. Her final message asked whether this had all been a scam the entire time, or if it had at any point meant something more to me. Thunderstorms rumbled nightly as the ice over the river melted and wild Petersburg summer approached once more. I myself did not know the answer to her question, and told her so. She never wrote to me again.

Throughout all this, Buffi's original profile had remained online, fixed in a state of digital innocence. Though I'd long since committed to memory her cropped photos and mild, sunny answers to questions about what was important in life, I'd gotten into the habit of checking her profile at least once a day: It seemed to me that the secret to reversing time, or at least to atonement, might still be embedded there. Then one morning in August Buffi erased it all. What remained was a single phrase she had entered under the "In Your Own Words" section. It read, simply, "Love is a social construct."

I knew then it was a baleful lie. I stared at the words till they went blurry, as though I were trying to parse out the individual pixels of which they were composed. And for a moment (though it could have been my mind playing tricks on me) I thought I did see them as they were—floating, discreet, each on its own just an incoherent little bundle of darkness and light— before I laid my head down on the keyboard and wept.

# ALCESTIS, BOUND
Paul Franz

Comedy is about the presentness of the present, as measured by its subtraction and repayment. Sometimes repayment with interest—though always with a measure of pain. The excess measures our desire for the present, which comedy makes manifest, or brings into being.

What is the relationship between poignancy and the comic? The poignancy of the comic is not in accord with the word's root. For the poignancy of the comic does not stab; it is, rather, an experience of tension. It is a limit placed in the middle of the world, not at the edge of the world. It is a limit beyond which is also life.

What is the difference between yearning and desire? Desire, we are told, seeks possession. Yearning seems to seek rather proximity. The physiology of yearning: is it not something that grabs you in the mid-section—that is, around the stomach—and pulls you forward? Yearning can, it is true, mount towards the throat. Perhaps, as yearning approaches the throat, it approaches desire. For desired parches. The boundary between yearning and desire would therefore seem to be around the middle of the esophagus. We are still not speaking about the loins—for they have no part in yearning, which does not, so to speak, "desire" possession. For yearning understands that possession is its limit, inasmuch as it dissolves the discreteness of the proximate objects.

Hence love is a matter of yearning. Hence the distance implicit in love. And this distance is the matter of comedy, how it insists on holding us at bay, throughout and especially at its endings. It is said that comedy ends with incorporation, the reintegration of the formerly sundered community; but death is the true incorporation: the consummate matter of tragedy. Comedy, the truest comedy—Alcestis returned from the tomb, but mortal, silent; Hermione delivered by art without redress of the lost years, son lost but daughter found—ends by preserving tension, the tension of the tuned string.

Does comedy tighten or loosen its string by ending with the promise of children? And what about living happily ever after? As, indeed, Raunce and Edith at the end of Henry Green's Loving are said to do. Do we take this as a kind of apotheosis? Green's novel, one of the greatest modern comedies, is a novel from a time of war—the greatest war, then or since. From what vantage point, therefore, is its last line spoken? Is it spoken in hope, hence in agony? Or does it, delphic, reserve the possibility that "ever after" is not a long time? (Then, too, there is the silence about Raunce's Albert, gone off to the wars, determined to avenge himself—on misunderstandings.) Or does it consign the lovers to another realm, the realm of fable, from which we feel an agony of exclusion?

Wishes to have the dead awaken, inanimate become animate: no wonder comedy—*Alcestis*, *The Winter's Tale*, and, yes, *Loving*, its Albert playing at "blind man's buff," blinded by love—is so often peopled with statuary.

# VIVAMUS
Paul Franz

Shouts in the street; those bleary blue
Eyes rolling back in no head: pay
No heed. Whatever rafter lets
Its tresses down of termite dust

The trespassing assassin's step
Is headed for another door
Than ours. As once upon a time
We did, so now let doze

In its black crib the whole night through
That channel we did not pay
To receive: mealy-mouthed
Or mouthed with a fury of bees.

# B with Blue Drink
Ruby Sutton

"We're recording."

Let me tell you a story.

Let me tell you how people used to meet, in the beginning of the '80s, into the middle part of the '80s until the late '80s, when everybody started dropping like flies. It was the night of my thirtieth birthday. We had a small dinner party—there were maybe ten of us. I was walking home down West Broadway when the thought, or the feeling, came over me that I did not want to spend the night alone. It was the 27th of December and it was so cold. Luis was in Spain with his boyfriend at the time. We were together but we'd usually both have at least one boyfriend on the side, and until one of us got too jealous this suited us fine. Anyway, I decided I'd go home with the first person that looked at me. Hopefully he'd be decent looking. Two blocks later I saw a man who was a little bit taller than me, slender with a long stride. Thankfully he was more than decent looking. He told me his name was Giles. A Frenchman from Bordeaux, he was smart, inquisitive, worldly. Good energy. He asked if I would like to go home with him, his loft was just around the corner on Spring and West Broadway. I said yes.

The loft, it turned out, was not really his. Giles was a professional bohemian. Having gone to boarding school with French aristocrats, he had collected, over the years, an assortment of both old rich and newly wealthy friends whose houses he'd stay for free in, or in exchange only for his good luck and his charm and perhaps a few favors he didn't mention. That week he was staying in the home of the great-grandchild of the Earl of Rosslyn. The condition was that Giles uncrate the heavy mahogany Egyptian revival furniture his friend had sent from his country home and delivered to his brand-new Soho apartment.

There was one piece of unpacked furniture inside the entire loft: an orange velvet couch. So we broke the ice on it.

Giles invited me to a New Year's Eve party he was having—he did not like manual labor of any kind, and wanted something to look forward to after he finished his project. I guess it was four days later that the party happened. When I arrived, he had unpacked and there were antiques everywhere.

Antique rugs, antique lamps, antique furs, antique busts. Soon, there were all these people buzzing around the loft—interesting people, from all over, sitting under the chandelier lamps with cheetah furs thrown over their shoulders and Persian rugs under their toes. It was like visiting a small museum. We made ourselves at home. I was sitting on the sofa when the elevator door opened and out came a woman with the most amazing hairdo. It was sort of like a beehive. Back then, women usually had at least one gay guy who would do their hair. This woman came and sat down right next to me. She told me her name was B., sort of flirtatiously. Almost right away, we hit it off as kindred spirits. We spent the whole party talking on that couch, not so much about ourselves, but watching the people around. B. liked to make up stories. Oh, do you see the woman in the leopard print? She dumped her boyfriend this afternoon and is starting to regret it— that's why she's prowling around with a martini in her hands. Or, you see that man in the fedora? He likes to get tied up. By the woman in the pink coat. But his girlfriend doesn't know. That's why they're circling around the room, trying to avoid eye contact over the fruit platter. They were fantasies, I suppose.

    We stayed on that couch all night watching the room twirl, until B. pulled a pack of cards out of her purse and read my tarot. She said she'd do a simple three-card spread. The first card she flipped over had an image on it of a man hacking away at a coin with a hammer, very focused, intense. B. asked if I had done a lot of physical labor in my past. I said yes. In the middle, B. pulled out a card with two people holding hands with a rainbow above their heads. For my future, B. pulled out the Star card. A woman with one foot in the water, one on earth. She explained that the Star represented someone able to communicate between the material world and the spiritual. This is when B. looked me in the eyes and said we were very similar.

    B. would turn out to be a very pivotal person, in my life,

89

and, I think, in the lives of many others. In New York, some people were like galaxies, some were like stars and some were planets. It's hard to say what made someone a galaxy or a star as opposed to something smaller on the cosmological spectrum. Everyone, it seemed to me, had a whole lot of energy. But the stars and galaxies sucked you into their orbit.

B. and I exchanged phone numbers on the back of a napkin, and three days later I was at her apartment. She had a loft on Prince Street, with twelve windows looking out at the Empire State Building, where she would throw great big lavish dinner parties. Her apartment was something of a nest for kindred spirits, of just about every variety. Artists, musicians, hairdressers, hat makers. It was at B.'s loft that I would meet Basquiat, who was Samo then, and John Cage, who made great music you could hardly stand. I remember one party where B's mother came to dinner. It was B. on one end of the table, B.'s mother on the other, and about fifteen young men—all gay, and all very good looking — in between. About halfway through dinner, Lisa stood up and made a toast. She said, I'd like to thank you all for the excellent conversation this evening. And I'd especially like to thank my daughter B., thanks to whom I've met so many wonderful young men since I gave birth to her.

"How many years ago?!" Huck Snyder stood up and asked. We all laughed. B.'s age was always a mystery—whenever anyone asked, she giggled and said "guess." She must have been twenty years older than us because she had watched the modern art movement unfold. She'd seen Picasso's first show at the Museum of Modern Art, which was where she'd learned how to paint in the abstract. When she talked about her childhood, the story was always the same — she grew up in the South Bronx before the neighborhood had a name, living with her parents in a one-bedroom apartment across from an elevated train.

B. called herself a "high-creative," although her career never really took off, as we say, I guess. Her masterpiece was her collection of gay men. A scientist in the art of social engineering, she had a radar, and she knew what she was looking for. If you were at all interesting, and especially if you were good looking, she'd suck you in. Huck Snyder was B.'s best boyfriend. He'd do anything for her, even have sex with her—I mean this was back then. They would curate shows together, get in huge fights—one of them would call you in tears, the other would run off to California, and then two weeks later, you'd get a postcard from Berlin with their names signed next to each other's. It was on one of these trips to Germany that she posed for Nan Goldin. "B with blue drink" is the name of the piece. Staring coyly into the camera, with a big blue martini glass, while the boys behind her are whispering. Wearing big white sunglasses, so you can't really tell what she's thinking.

Having lived in New York all her life, B. had a sixth sense: she always knew where the next thing was happening. It was through her that I ended up going to the East Village galleries, and that I got my first show at Civilian Warfare, showing my cow paintings. Because of her I even started acting. She cast me as a tree in this performance art piece. It might have been 1982. 83. It's hard for me to remember the years but I'm really trying. She always made fun of my landscapes. Anything natural terrified her: moss, twigs, birth, disease. Birds — even though she looked like she could have been one of them. Anyway, when the mood started shifting, she was already in Miami.

"I don't do dates, like I told you already," B. told Daisy. "But it must have been sometime in the mid-80s. All I remember was thinking, it's not supposed to be this cold in February. Then I turned the corner onto Spring Street, and this breeze of cold wind just *slapped* me. I just thought, *I have to go*.

"So, yeah," she said, refilling her Coke, "That's how I sold the loft and ended up in Miami. I don't know what you mean by 'East Village art scene' or 'things happening.' I was just coming up with ideas, like I always am, like I'm still doing. I'm getting tired, so tell me. Is that what you came all the way down here to ask me?"

91

# From a novel in progress
Matthew Gasda

### 0:00

*such terrible things (a broken heart wishes for a new punishment) you
were growing wild like mint heartpressure long stresses of a future
Thou made alien in the body's longing and even without language I
am saying this that on the day of Ascension a million years from all
this will be forgotten this small human stuff extinguished by its own
heat (the fragrance of your mouth) decoherence the arrow of time point
everywhere in a complex adaptive system I'm swimming against
the grain of branching histories playing a game of dice these random
fluctuations give rise to what you see on the screen it all depends on the
condition of taste so you must weigh the violence with your hands the
Gothic inventor does not leave a sign of his interpretation and makes
the fire as real as he can self-organizing meanings St John's Passion it
only comes alive in certain moments honestly as it stands right now*

### 0:36

*like an aria arguing against the end of the song cinema is a random
walk through memories and desires tracking the progressive destruc-
tion of a relationship and other things at that a fundamental level
we could never see because an organism does not want to become
punishable devouring myself I cannot stop the camera loves watching
shadows there's something intricate in the editing process that reminds
of the way I rearrange myself until I can't be any other way (from
the beginning of my life I experienced acute humiliation which was
my true talent retaining all the reactions of the people who watched
and noticed me) experience teaches us how to counter our own feelings
with symbols even if the words are ignored all sorts of phantom limbs
will sprout through the stump of silence new chains of association
form retrace the original meanings elliptical can't explain where these
moments come from I don't know what this film is about the camera is
out of track still lingering pushing beyond the barrier of her eyes like
a fish venturing beneath the pressurized zone of warm water into the
depths where the monsters swim conditioned to accept this shame as
predicate you come back to it always watching yourself unsure of how*

*many instances of your own life have yet to arrive you were asleep a*
*kind of machine (a great happiness stunned and a mirror broken) it's*
*all there the rainstorm and your bad mood and Charlie Byrd playing*
*guitar the nucleus of a universe has formed around the lens each image*
*holds what you were thinking walking back from the farmer's mar-*
*ket holding a paper bag of meat and vegetables so much had changed*
*foredark of the autumn evening (we got there just in time)*

### 0:58

*saturn smoke darkness sleep is beautiful like uncoiled hair uprooted*
*God suddenly in the dark like being dead are you rising just as the*
*imagination rises differentiating itself from dream restless energy a*
*violet sea free of close entanglements bypassing parents ancestors cul-*
*ture ordinary things Freud said a dream is a little psychosis an auton-*
*omous product a psyche with purpose he's making coffee in the kitchen*
*she's looking through his records looking up as if there's a skylight you*
*reach your arms out I come towards you like thawing water towards*
*you transplant the future into the past the fire of the eyes is the last*
*to go out half lost along the way looking looking for what you were*
*after gone in the morning you have to memorize her body the frag-*
*ments of the world aligned the crushed eroticism like flower petals  the*
*heart emits a sign that the camera captures and seals imprisoning the*
*circumstance*

### 1:01

*create and to recreate create a figure release from the foreground you*
*make the trivia of events relevant by giving them perspective context*
*frame remember return revise reflect recognition is knowledge coming*
*from what is already in the soul react repeating going back repenting*
*remorse religious words linking or tying back (and this is what our*
*dreams are doing and our memories bringing us to respect ourselves)*

### 1:23

*they must ruthlessly persecute each other with annihilatory rhetoric a*
*character with a dynamic power of acting upon the audience he places*
*his hand on her sternum kisses her neck they aren't speaking but there*
*is still a logical path forward from the finite to the infinite in a second*

93

*of cinema there are a relentless series of decisions to be made unmas-*
*tered unconceited intact flowers uncut in their vases I realized that*
*cruelty is normal in unloved crooked people like us making needlework*
*out of the moonlight rainghosts kingfishers building their nests I make*
*another cut here*

1:58

*slow-moving reflections on the relationship between memory and*
*selfhood photography and history and my mother's eyes dying into*
*nighttime are you asleep I'm only dreaming*

2:01

*his hands close around her throat and she can't feel what's happening*
*it's like she's asleep he could kill her and she wouldn't mind a sober-*
*ing portrayal of a young woman's unsatisfactory affairs the technical*
*solution to each problem to come to me intuitively without any pre-*
*conceptions obedience to touch floats down from the rafters wanting*
*something as real as the unreal was at first losing its essential struc-*
*ture like a virus the script tells us there is nothing that can save you*
*from catastrophic losses which pile up like bad investments the focus is*
*pulled suddenly the world melts eyes open deadset against dreaming*
*for too long we know ourselves through the activity and performance*
*of the body the field upon which the soul explores itself half alive in the*
*bomb shelter of the heart dancing a tango on your hands every radical*
*grievance hides the shame of having been conquered into the bedroom*
*tugging at her shoulders made of earth and longing anoint her fore-*
*head there's something almost fatherly about it yet she's almost thirty*
*why isn't she a mother he pulls at her dress she knows the routine*
*aimless yet part of the strictest system of discipline you often make the*
*audience unexpectedly adjust the levels of their involvement the tone*
*of certain characterizations and the apparent disinterest of the cam-*
*era as it records events create an atmosphere of distances between the*
*characters and their world action and repetition a kind of ritualism*
*the intimacy of juxtaposition comes from the risk of the images can-*
*nibalizing each other we want to believe that what lies beneath the*
*strangeness and incomprehensibility of the persona is inert and won't*
*hurt us but we're lying to ourselves lines have appeared around her*

*eyes it's driving her crazy*

## 2:50

*dramaturgy based on distance distance is based on hope hope based on eroticism or escaping from the consumerist world spiritualizing the body he turns the lights on and off around her watching but there is no longer any point to it something's missing they're in a degraded state fallen or falling or both*

## 2:58

*greeneyes in the eveningdark he touches her but she feels nothing not even aroused he touches her again the camera pulls forward as if part of the process of seduction (and yet we have to believe that no one is watching)*

## 3:33

*every moment pulls me deeper and deeper into the tomb or womb of my own art the mirror image is all I have of the original self (a blind shell-fish opening up exposing its body to all the small fish playing about it in order to lure them in and crush them between its valves take)*

## 4:56

*from the dark fires cut the skin to the bone the dominant idiom is naturalism punctuated with what lies beyond and leaks through loneliness follow them simply waiting for the ax to fall entropy or dispersal of order only in this intensity is there grace what have I made other than a sacrifice touching together the extreme disclosures of withdrawal into the world of bodily configurations you can still hear intellectual melodies or resonances I've become so cold I can barely bring myself to regret the love I tortured into an arcana of drives and unauthorized encounters drinking too much I thought that meant being free mourning a world which has been nailed to the cross written fast and only now reconstructing what it was I haven't told you the half of it how hamstrung this inherent power was this coercive illusion along the spine there is enough fertility to produce endlessly its generative when you have a trope of a higher order you can participate in a new kinds*

*of creation trying to count the rabbits bolting out of the warren white-*
*stones in the grassblades sweet pliable coherence no turtles or founda-*
*tions these images rest on nothing hyperaware that we're at the end*
*of history (like a car that has run out of road speeding a million miles*
*an hour) she wants a cigarette he hands her one cut here at another*
*beautiful object mark a place for them in the magnetic field of Bach's*
*music pulmonary milkbright stars long filaments of futurity you will*
*spend this time alone the Earth needs a mirror I think floating above*
*it dangling from a satellite*

### 5:12

*we keep recording the hollowness of their bodies looking for the mo-*
*mentous expectation of sex in my own relentless opposition to myself I*
*can't seem to find a way to be amidst semi-impossible obligations and*
*the subsequent breakdowns of the logical and syntactical apparatus the*
*brain heaves forward stimulated by self-talk and desire on a planet*
*increasingly volatile and inhuman the D minor derelict hands incor-*
*porate a fragment of the splintering pain of birth your mother's cries*
*your head crowning the fissures that let the world in this struggle to*
*create an image grows under the snow a bulb that shoots up sudden-*
*ly and dies just as quick metaphors fall into rank the script is just a*
*point of departure we disembark from the shores of reason deep now*
*in the psyche where nothing escapes but what is most overwhelming I*
*can experience the pleasure of merely circulating through aisthesis like*
*poison in the blood look how far away they've gotten you sculpt from*
*the long block of eternity you try to make a moment my eyes hurt my*
*neck is sore a pattern is whatever you truly insist on tenuous moments*
*begin to communicate across the fragments swimming downstream*
*from last year when you sat in my window brushing your hair it keeps*
*flashing the sun on the earth the radiance of its glance the systems*
*networks codes that address You the nothing of the opening the onto-*
*logical roof that's leaking(adoration)sinking beneath the imagination's*
*floor and floating above its rafters flesh materializes inside the symbol*
*is miraculous the way something artificial becomes self-embodying and*
*extraordinarily real (teasing apart the cathedral of the nerves) it feels*
*like a wound but it might be a miracle born very late in the duskland*
*(you are unlocalizable outside the world)*

96

## 5:33

*pulling up the stalks of meaning begin another scene phosphorescence
the daystar climbing through the trees outside my window Eros and
imagination are a single motion of the same general action where
the whole question of behavior is swept in and out of view there's so
much in the irregularity of the daily unbecoming that you launch into
the near-term future you are monotone I am imperfect and along the
circles of the farsweeping shore there is a sharp expression of God's
work as interesting as it is dull (we must resist and decompose) live
the rest of my life in remorse like Lear 24 frames per second such as it
is (motionless and alive) partition the heart into chambers I started
to cry drank the water of life floated back to the surface bright slender
gold thrice-lost love of my life I held you like a child it is not my fault
new waves of inspiration are flowing in like lights seen from space I
see your eyes and only now have I remembered (the ruin of houses and
cities on fire) and it's a very long way back gathering the fragments
of the world like flowers the stories of so many lives and deaths (the
coldness in people and the shame of having lived this way for too long)
skin of your heart and the heat of your breath (you pity us and I feel
ashamed) long stretches of silence cover the earth like grass*

## 5:58

*he pulls his hands into his lap kisses on the cheek holds her against his
body the beginning of the film is the end of them (or is it?) it's hard
to tell how far along the decay is or how far it can extend into the
directionless infinity of their lives you could take this moment and
chop it into smaller and smaller pieces until there was nothing there
fundamentally I think I've failed to cross the distances having fallen
for this paradox and in the last revelation I heard the beginning of the
sweetness kind of truth (the one you whisper) it was late at night you
were crying (I wrote that in too) and does anyone except you recognize
how the basic parameters of speech have been reworked into imagery I
took your words joint by joint I parted the*

### 6:02

*gradually as if rising from the ground a new anxiety takes the place of the old in the next scene it is raining but we're not there yet she's still inside his house (she's still his) it's as if they were always there*

### 7:55

*(the texture the mind feels crossing a threshold)it is the interiority which is most lacking and you feel it just as it begins pushing through you taught as metaphor itself (primordial sight and then grace in no particular order) and I don't think loneliness has to refrain from speaking we should listen to it more create poetic and cinematic enclosures in which what remains can truly remain (a disruption of the ecotropological balance) nothing but what you've already surrendered and what might in the long run have disappeared forever in the desert of the heart statements unravel turn back upon themselves it is my eyesight going that worries me there's something unspeakable in blindness and what does it mean to survive over time and disorder at the creative junction where something miraculous happens where the mind can still emerge out of the shallows to fuse the ruptures of image into cinema the images that otherwise would leak through and destroy the speechspace (aerial shipwrecks visible fire a city burning from the inside out)*

### 8:05

*what are they doing in this modern world last membrane punctured by doubt and desire and grief shucked from stars an anemone blooming inconsequential in its beauty after so long you see the last planet rotating on its sphere the camera tends to lapses the cuts create specters and analogies (levels) where the future is buried like the corpse of a father or brother*

### 8:15

*always until the last (a searching) as I remember you were there there was no one and we were waiting but that was nothing I forget*

## 8:17

*something undoes us the cutting of the last frame produces a contrast as strange as summer lightning you could almost believe it was something special like something divine you could believe there was a force behind or beneath (but there is nothing) you could believe but you don't you could*

## 10:02

*now into the end of nature past the first point of beginning there structure of a film is prophetic receptivity is a semantic aim I feel like a rock out at sea people surge around me he's telling her about his dream but he's lying I was lying the halftruth of the full truth becomes clear when you spell it out this way*

## 12:03

*cheap red wine on the floor he's trying to integrate himself in*

# Toothpaste or Birdsong
Aaron Fagan

Hypnosis of the swan begins with the routine technique
Of fixing the gaze. Governments collapse as mountains
And rivers rise. Tonight, a high wind gathers intensity.
Soft rime frost forms on evergreens in the aftermath,
And strangers pass us by one after another for a lark.
May love saturate your years and let your memories,
Innocent of loss, conspire in such a way you'll not
Be sure it was real—hard to say and harder to write.
Curtains part, you enter fleeing the hollow promise
Of the human race and exit, pursued, without a trace.
Long separations from the people you love to hate
Reverse affections and detestations with gloss and blur.
That first judgment was not the end of the matter,
But the first word still reveals us erratic fields of force.


# Heat Wave
Aaron Fagan

It is only because the inner region is hotter
Than the outer region that the sun does not
Collapse under its own gravity, to be sure,
Like logic keeping an accord of what makes
Making a way through things independent
Of its catalog of definite details jailed in
Certainties from so long ago for the sake
Of taking the sky out of a mourning dove
To sing an appreciation of planned clarity
In the voice of the storm it travels through
With the sparkling aura of an emissary—
The fever dream renounces its night music,
Desire grips the clear promise of a dead
Giveaway we will never know by the signs.

# Horse-Cock Sandwich

Aaron Fagan

You died making money for someone else,
And more died making money for you—
You are not the best and not the worst.
Homes with sun-bleached prints of famous
Paintings crowd the walls of every room
Starved of all sincerity. And this just shows
To go you, you were dead long before
You died. In a rare, unspeakable moment
You tried to point out how my face melts
Away from me twice each day, and yet,
The two of us here together again remains
Abductive, lost in space until the square
Circles and goes back to the green room
Where we ask when not *where* are you?


# The Country Builder's Assistant

Aaron Fagan

While pressed for time here, I want you to talk
To me until you understand what you mean.
I know something is going to happen but not what.
For the sake of the planet, let's just eat each other,
And get it over with. Asher Benjamin stole more
About classical orders and academic style than
Anything original in *The Country Builder's Assistant*.
"You should get a job making people nervous!"
As Charles Manson used to say, but here we are,
Left in the dust of our inventions with an army
Of teenagers laughing high as testimony through
The cemetery, playing war with Roman candles
Over a bottle of peach schnapps in November,
The penultimate month with no imagination.

# The Zebra Lounge
Aaron Fagan

Debbie the bartender is drunk and showing off
The lamb-shaped pound cake she made for Easter—
Back legs broken and soaked with Grand Marnier.
Last week, she was studying from her *Gray's Anatomy*
Then turned it in her lap for me to inspect its scale
Diagram of the female reproductive system, tapping
A spot on the page asking: "What's the glans clitoris?"
I turned and wrote: The bar dog, looking starved,
Got tired of loyalty. Tommy the pianist always says,
"Time is fun when you're having flies." He only plays
The opening chords of "Bennie and the Jets" and stops,
Which never fails to piss people off. If a tourist dares
To make a request, he mondegreens the lyrics to insults
Every regular comes to know better than the originals.


# An Autumn Afternoon
Aaron Fagan

All that lasts is what was done for no reward,
Which is to say very little. Very little, indeed.
Just give an honest picture of what went on,
Is that so much to ask? There was Tall Paul,
Who was tall, and Overall Paul, who was tall,
Too, but as one might infer, wore only overalls.
One of them said, *I don't know what's wrong
With you, but it shows*, but I can't remember who.
I want to lie about smoking on the floor all day—
Zippo and Chesterfields by my side as I stare up
At the ceiling, one arm free to cradle my head
As I glance over at the bookshelves from time
To time, lost in memories of what I remember
Of what I have read about what others had to say.

# My Eye Is Stuck, so Is My Language
Aaron Fagan

I ask why owls are important
And think it's a good question
To ask. Face the world as it is
And not as we would have it be.
After I was dead, I saw I was no
Longer alive. The future of past
Perfect fails to teach: *All for each
And each for all.* I accept all art
Is humiliation. Whether I like
It or not, this is how the voice
In my head sounds mixed deep
In paper pools of bloodletting.
But before you sing my song
It must first be burnt to ashes.


# All Good People Are a Sleeping Painting
Aaron Fagan

Had I known what love was, I would have paid you
As much attention as I paid your tea trying not
To spill it as I walked across the room to you,
Although I might have paid attention differently.
Fear's provenance is an essential fiction, and I am
A lotus eater blissed out with awe without it.
We all lie under oath, competing at love and death,
But it lends to an order in the ecstasy of chaos, pain,
And joy rolled into one scattered dream of history,
While actual history is unwritten at daybreak—
We explore infinite will at the hayrake table,
The animal kingdom in us comes out from hiding
To hunt and be hunted down. I took a shine
To you when others said I was wrong to trust you.

# Love, Money & Fitness
Aaron Fagan

In his night-haunted daydream, he felt his way around silence,
Recognition, and the common senses that were the error
Of his leanings, just as the known path is now unknown,
Such that his habits, a shoal of bream, are eager to surrender
The whole flash aspect of a waning gibbous moon. He tries
Once more, again, and fails to rest until he can fail for more.
Explore the pace. Put an ear to your lover's heart and dial
The nipple back and forth like a safecracker. Looking down
At the paper, it says a body dripping blood was found along
With a small fortune on board a cargo jet. Otherwise, its lies
Have made us whole. It's been brave to walk around in shorts
At this time of year, seeing how cold it is. I will catch my death.
I am because I say I am. Eyes closed, he feels the heat fade from
His body. She slowly entered the room but arrived all at once.


# Vega Once and Again North Star
Aaron Fagan

Birds aren't real, but magic beans are. In a world brimming
With trust, unarmed to the teeth and staged to blossom,
A realistic attitude might be to consider death as an imperative
Need. Being made in the museum of gradual decay sounds
Like it means more than it does. Meanwhile, Milton blazes
By the cops as he bombs down Dictionary Hill. Utopia means
No place, which is to say either impossible or decentralized.
Lost-wax casting these cranky temporalities, at the garage
Getting stuff other mechanics fucked up fixed, stuff I could fix
If I had access to the right tools, but I don't, so *The Price Is Right*
Is on television, and it reminds me a little of when I was little,
How it used to fill me with such joy when someone won a car,
It made me think of how much their lives would be improved.
Fuck all that is free in an unfree world full of campus novels.

# A Preface to Screwed and Chopped Logic

Aaron Fagan

Coming in last is my specialty in this new life without you.
I love classical mechanics. The ingenuity of the oppressed
Always seems to impress people. The room is established
In an overtly ornamental way, posing for humanity as one.
If I were a fashion shoot, would I be enough? All puckered
Lips and contempt for the labyrinthine desires I inspire?
Forget the unfinished quatrain where Yeats may or may
Not lie for quasi-eternity. Does it mean for us to question
Whether we are meant to pass by—or stop and think?
Caveat lector, and all the rest. Being everyone's anyone
Is a short course in calculus. The personality of god will
Wear out your heart of hearts as rays rake across the heart
Of 14th Street which once appeared to us but a silver mist,
Substance where it suspected only a confusion of sorrows.

# Educations
Jackson Frons

The poet wasn't her favorite poet, but she figured he was someone's. He had a reputation. His work was referential and hard to parse. When he read aloud, the language sounded musical. Presiding over her workshop, he was bashful. He corrected himself. He gently engorged the egos of the aspiring poets the way you might feed carrots to a horse. "This part sings," he said. "What's going on here? I like what's going on here. What's in the shadows."

She'd seen the poet daily for a week now and noted, each time he entered the room, how his eyes shadowed her. He had pale blue piteous eyes that were shrouded by limp, red skin. They were eyes he seemed guilty of. Guilt, really, was the poet's main thing. Only charming, effortless people had the luxury of guilt.

Her poems weren't good, but they were elusive, which made them interesting, she thought. That was more than she could say for most contemporary work. She was getting older, stringy-er. Her fillings were oxidizing. Her hair didn't shine. She was one of those people who'd aged into herself. She could no longer imagine herself young. Pictures of her from then looked foreign and false. She looked at them sometimes at night and tried to remember how it had felt being that way.

Her youth was murky—odd jobs and bursts of psychosis. A summer at the outlets in Camarillo, a few years in the desert—turquoise, leather, etc.—and, before she'd moved back east for good, there was one odd winter she'd lived in Chatsworth and read people their fortunes over the phone. Sometimes men called the line and she'd hear the rumpled sound of them jacking off. "Write that," the poet said. He meant the part with the men. He shook the pages until they hummed. "Put all that in here."

This was on the final day of the workshop, which was held at a writer's conference, really more of a camp for adults. They shared an afternoon coffee, seated in Adirondack chairs, shaded by a large coniferous tree.

Before them: grass crested with vibrant yellow weed-flowers. Quaint wooden buildings. People ambling by, blind to the excruciating brightness of it all. She had a headache and her stomach hurt and she did not know the last time she'd had any water.

"I very much like your poems," the poet said. "They show great promise."

She itched at her nose.

"I don't want you to be upset by this," the poet adjusted himself. "Your work must become more radical. More traditional as well. More traditional and more radical at once. You need to get in the mud, then make the mud translucent."

"Translucent mud. Interesting."

The very idea of what a poem was felt so slippery. It was possible that this sensation was actually what she liked about poetry.

The poet wore a hat made of straw. His face was peripherally wrinkled. He described his work as a nervous system of sound.

Her face was flat and long. She felt ancient.

"I hate my poems," she said.

"No, no," he said. "This isn't a cause for self-recrimination."

"No," she said. "That's not what I mean."

"You seem depressed," the poet said.

She wasn't happy. She knew that. But she also knew she wasn't any one thing. She was a collection of not-things.

"I'm not happy," she said

"And you are married?" the poet said.

"Yes."

The poet hunched and gripped his knees. She thought he was looking for something on the ground. Then she thought that he was having a heart attack.

"Perhaps, and this is just my own impulsive, intrusive thought…Perhaps you should maybe consider getting unmarried."

"*Un*-married," she said. "Hmm."

107

"I'm very sorry," the poet said. "That was wrong to suggest."

The poet emailed her a few weeks later. She was at home with her husband and did not want to open it in front of him. They kept a small, simple house. He was handy. What she liked about him was this: he'd grown up poor and he was sincere.

Her husband scarfed his morning cereal. The milk clung in his bristly facial hair. She hated milk. It disgusted her. She subsisted mostly on dried fruit and nuts and apple sauce. Out the window, a school bus collected brightly dressed children. She'd been an embarrassed child. Now children embarrassed her. Her younger sister's child, even. Once, she'd been watching TV with the child in her lap when it pointed at the weatherman and said, "Is he 200 years old?"

She adjuncted a 4/4 load of composition at an ungainly state institution. Her students were dim and ungrateful. Based on her reviews, they hated her, too.

Some excerpts from the last semester:

*- I truly think I have never had a worse impression of a professor.*

*- She is shy but also condescending and disrespectful.*

*- A pretty nice women (sic); however, she is a terrible teacher.*

*-Her class is extremely boring and her assignments are so unclear. She does not have a good rubric for her papers and doesn't even know what she wants from students.*

*- Hopefully with time she will get better.*

She was meant to teach a theoretical curriculum. One designed not only to prepare the students to write across academic disciplines, but, also, to inculcate them into the pedagogical study of writing and the specific language of this study. She found it moronic. The terms were impenetrable, the assignments pointless. And, more conceptually, you could write, or study writing, but you couldn't study the act of writing. This was as vacuous as people who talked about their dreams.

The students were meant to receive heuristics and reflect

on their exigence—ideally, in a multi-modal fashion. Instead, she read them poems. Poems that they ignored. So she proffered worksheets about the poems. She cut the poems up and asked them to reorder the lines. While they pretended to work, she took deliberate, extended excursions to the bathroom. She liked the windows there. They were made from rough privacy glass and only allowed light and soft, shadowy shapes to pass through. She operated with little scrutiny.

Sometimes she took a section to the University's public art gallery. She kept the worksheets printed and on file.

"We're going to the gallery," she'd announce, then walked them there under the cement sky with their amassed silence waked behind her.

She wandered the gallery alone, pausing to watch them scribble. If any of them looked like they were preparing to ask her a question, she'd try to escape. Their questions were somehow both extremely stupid and totally unanswerable. *What was the poet thinking when he wrote this? Which of the paintings is the best one?*

Eventually the class departed and she was left alone.

She stood before a canvas that was abstract with the exception of one small corner, that contained a miniaturized, detailed urban skyline. The rest of the painting was a blur—streaks of blue and orange. It was a painting the poet emailed her about.

What, exactly, did he expect her to like here. Was she supposed to identify with a specific element? Students were always talking about relating to things. Was she expected to "relate?"

Maybe she related to the tiny people in those buildings gazing out upon the mess of color amassing outside. Or was the blue-orange stuff meant to be the mud that she was supposed to be making translucent. Or maybe this mud already was translucent…

She continued to stare at the painting until it took on a watery texture and each brush stroke almost revealed itself. It was like a poem—read it enough times and the poet appears behind the work. What would happen if she returned to this painting everyday and stared at it like this. This was the type of endured devotion to art that writers she'd read about performed. There was something like this in a novel. A man digs himself out of a jail cell only to find himself in another jail cell. Something to that effect. A sound echoed somewhere. She blinked a few times and assessed the room. It was symmetrical and sanitary. There was one artwork on each wall.

She photographed the canvas and the placard that listed its title, artist, and dimensions. She emailed the images to the poet.

When she saw the photo of the painting later, it no longer interested her.

She didn't tell her husband about the poet. Had he asked who she was always typing to, she would have lied. When she thought about this—lying—it felt like her finger nails might slide off or that just a few of her bones had turned liquid.

They were not always long or substantive emails. The poet cataloged his daily tasks. His fears about his life—it being mostly over.

*My work is irregular. The new book, the sequence, is a mess. I'm getting a cancer screening. I'm not sure what part of me it is this time, but I can't eat for almost a day. I'm sure it will work itself out.*

She stuck to things she saw—a good sunset, a row of matching houses, poems, an old Toyota pickup (a red one, banded with shining chrome).

She also included pictures of herself. In one, taken with the self-timing camera on her computer, she looked surprised.

There were days she didn't hear from the poet. She spent those days waiting, anxiously. It wasn't that she was waiting to read his email, but for the chance to write her own email back to him. Writing to the poet was thrilling and clarifying. It made her want to wake up early and write by hand. She kept the finished notebooks in a stack by her bed. Her poems, lately, were addressed to some anonymous others. They were not to the poet. She didn't know who they were. It was good that there was something left to figure out.

She told her husband she was going to visit a friend from the conference. He didn't question her. She wished he had. That would've given her a sense of clarity. It would've surprised her. She felt horrible about what she was doing. She packed basic clothes and wore unfortunate shoes.

The poet looked up and down as he read. Not many people came. A few faculty members and a collection of preening students. It was a different University that, in all of its average-ness and gray, resembled her university.

He read from his newest book. He considered it an epic. "A sonic epic," he'd said in an interview.

The poems moved her more than she'd expected. The chair she sat in was padded and comfortable. The seat hinged like the ones in a movie theater and the lights were dimmed, which, even with the sun streaming in, gave the occasion a less surgically academic appearance.

She held an open copy of the book in her lap and followed along with him.

She waited for him in the lobby of the hotel. How long, she wasn't sure. Her husband texted her *safe?* She'd said: *safe*.

Time gets hard when it's like that.

It was the type of place where you knew the rooms were all identical. Even the pictures on the walls. Stripes of red and blue. A woman descending stairs to a beach.

"I'd like to watch you," he said as they undressed each other. He moved her hands off of him. "Show me your bliss."

And she did, for a while. It was only partly satisfying. She would've liked for him to just grab her.

She said, "I'm so hungry."

The poet put on the complimentary robe. He un-looped the belt and slung it over his shoulders. There was white hair on his chest and protruding green veins, like the borders on a map.

"You've not eaten?" he said. "I'm so sorry. Let me order

you something. What can I get you?"

She ate her orange chicken feverishly, hunched at the desk beside the television.

"Is it good?" the poet said.

She said, "Terrible. The viscosity of the sauce is horrifying."

"I'm sorry," he said. "I'm not sure how we handle all this. We can get something else, would that be better?"

"What?" she said. "No. I'm eating it. I just mean in the objective sense it's shitty."

"In a certain mood," the poet said.

"Yeah," she said. "A certain mood."

"Everything in a certain mood."

She cracked her knuckles. "I've had enough." She got in bed, beneath the plush covers.

"How are your poems?" the poet said.

"More radical," she said. "More traditional and more radical at once."

"That's not something you say. That's something someone tells you."

"What is it I say?"

"You're the only one with the fortune. I'm still waiting for my poem about that."

She fluffed the pillow.

"There was something there,"

"I could never understand."

"What's there not to understand?"

"Why?" she said. "When you can't even see."

"Why not," he said. "I mean, what other reason would a man have to dial into a thing like that."

The poet told her in the morning that he had a train. His wife was expecting him.

"You have a wife?" she said.

"And you have a husband."

His phone rang. He went into the hall to answer it. She turned through the pages of her notebook.

An hour later, he still hadn't come back. She went out to look for him. She called his name down the colonnade of identical doors. She went all the way to the elevator. He was nowhere.

It was then she realized she'd not taken a key. The door to their room, somewhere back down the hall, was locked.

She slumped down against the wall and let herself slide to the floor. If she was going to break down and cry, this would be the time to do it. It was a thin, pointless cry. She thought it was dumb. The tears collected at her chin. She held her face but that didn't do anything.

She went down to the lobby, past the concierge desk, and out to the street. She was barefoot.

Students lived in the neighborhood. It was the type of day where everyone young went outside. They looked just like her students—angular and sleek like dolphins. What did the poet think of when he looked at her? Did he see some luscious animal?

She thought of being a teenager. One time she rode the bus. Not a local bus. The type of bus that goes between cities. She'd gotten off the bus and, while walking into the depot amongst the crowd, she sensed that someone was watching her. It was a man—middle aged, in a rain slicker—seated on a bench with a duffle waiting between his legs like a dog. They made eye contact. She dissolved into the crowd.

This was it.

She hadn't been able to locate what exactly it was that interested her about this memory before.

Then she saw the poet on the sidewalk.

He carried a pink box. The type pastries come in. He had on a perfect, general expression. It was the face of someone waving from the deck of a receding ferry. The smile two lovers make when driving together on a lush highway, both of them looking straight ahead.